Optimizing Citrix® XenDesktop® for High Performance

Successfully deploy XenDesktop® sites for a high performance Virtual Desktop Infrastructure (VDI)

Craig Thomas Ellrod

BIRMINGHAM - MUMBAI

Optimizing Citrix® XenDesktop® for High Performance

First published: December 2015

Production reference: 1181215

Published by Packt Publishing Ltd.
Livery Place
35 Livery Street
Birmingham B3 2PB, UK.

ISBN 978-1-78528-768-8

www.packtpub.com

Notice

Some of the images in the chapters are taken from the Citrix website and documentation.

Credits

Author
Craig Thomas Ellrod

Reviewers
Erik Bakker
Rene Lindeboom
Jan Hendrik Meier
Florian Zoller

Commissioning Editor
Zeeyan Pinheiro

Acquisition Editor
Tushar Gupta

Content Development Editor
Zeeyan Pinheiro

Technical Editor
Dhiraj Chandanshive

Copy Editor
Kevin McGowan

Project Coordinator
Suzanne Coutinho

Proofreader
Safis Editing

Indexer
Priya Sane

Graphics
Kirk Rocque D'Penha

Production Coordinator
Nitesh Thakur

Cover Work
Nitesh Thakur

About the Author

Craig Thomas Ellrod has more than 25 years of experience in the computer industry and holds a bachelor's of science degree in computer science from California State University, Chico, and a master's in business administration from Pepperdine University. He has held many positions in the computer industry, including software programmer, support engineer, field and corporate system engineer, technical marketing manager, product marketing manager, and product manager. He has worked for companies such as Celerity Computing, Emulex, Pinnacle Micro, Sync Research, Cisco Systems, Citrix Systems®, Extreme Networks, and other smaller start-up ventures.

Craig currently works for Akamai as a solutions engineer and system architect in the Rockies region of the USA. He has authored patent applications and patent designs and received an innovation award while at Extreme Networks. Craig is passionate about technical marketing. He has written many deployment guides and is well versed in all Citrix® products. He also wrote a book on technical marketing, authored a XenApp® 6.5 video series, and wrote a book on *Getting Started with XenDesktop® 7.x*, *Packt Publishing*.

About the Reviewers

Erik Bakker is a freelance consultant/architect based in the Netherlands with a strong focus on Microsoft and Citrix® virtualization technologies (SBC and VDI). He is specialized in designing and troubleshooting large Citrix® and Microsoft environments using the latest available technologies.

He's been adept at Citrix® since the early WinFrame product and has since been certified in the complete Citrix suite up to the latest released products as an CCE-V for XenDesktop® 7.6. Besides working with the product, he's also a subject matter expert for Citrix regarding the Citrix® Virtualization Exams in which he helps to design the final exams.

Next to everything related to Citrix®, he's also an expert in Microsoft technologies. He has a broad knowledge of almost every Microsoft product released and is also certified in all major Microsoft products as an MCSE/MCITP.

Erik can be contacted on Twitter using the @bakker_erik handle or by sending him a message using LinkedIn at https://nl.linkedin.com/in/bakker123.

Rene Lindeboom lives in Almere, Netherlands, together with his wife and two little dogs.

He is (and has been for the last 15 years) a specialist in the fields of server-based computing, Virtual Desktop Infrastructures, and related application delivery technologies. He is also skilled in VMWare View, Horizon, and end user computing technologies such as Citrix® XenMobile®, RES Workspace Manager, and others.

Rene works for Platani Nederland as a senior IT specialist and is experienced in designing, implementing, and troubleshooting or reviewing larger customer environments based upon a sound and pragmatic approach. He likes transferring knowledge to those eager to get acquainted with new technologies and is fascinated by the speed in which technology evolves in this fast-moving world.

Platani Nederland offers specialized knowledge and expertise in all current technologies, delivered to the customer by experienced senior consultants in a quality-driven fashion using lessons learned and common sense. Find out more at `http://www.platani.nl`.

Follow Rene on Twitter at `@renelindeboom` or see his LinkedIn profile at `http://nl.linkedin.com/in/renelindeboom`.

Jan Hendrik Meier has more than 10 years of experience in IT. He started as a trainee for an IT-specialist company. During this time, he had his first contact with products from Microsoft and Citrix®. Now, he is an expert in infrastructure and virtualization solutions. In the Citrix® area, he started to work with an early XenDesktop® (or better XenApp) version—MetaFrame XP. He deepened his knowledge in the following products: Presentation Server, XenApp®, and XenDesktop® and started to expand this with knowledge about various other Citrix® products such as Provisioning Server, NetScaler®, and XenMobile®.

He is currently working as an IT architect for a medium-sized company based in Germany.

Furthermore, he writes books and professional articles on different IT technologies. If he finds interesting problems during his job, he writes description and solutions for them on his blog, which can be found at `http://www.jhmeier.de`.

> I wish my daughter Evi an awesome and wonderful life. May all her wishes be fulfilled.

Florian Zoller works as a lead IT architect at msg services, a consulting company based in Germany. He has several years of experience in designing and implementing Citrix® infrastructures for midsize and large customers. Besides his expert knowledge of XenApp®/XenDesktop®, XenMobile®, and Netscaler®, he focuses on software distribution and automation technologies such as Heat software desktop and server management, PowerShell, and so on.

www.PacktPub.com

Support files, eBooks, discount offers, and more

For support files and downloads related to your book, please visit www.PacktPub.com.

Did you know that Packt offers eBook versions of every book published, with PDF and ePub files available? You can upgrade to the eBook version at www.PacktPub.com and as a print book customer, you are entitled to a discount on the eBook copy. Get in touch with us at service@packtpub.com for more details.

At www.PacktPub.com, you can also read a collection of free technical articles, sign up for a range of free newsletters and receive exclusive discounts and offers on Packt books and eBooks.

https://www2.packtpub.com/books/subscription/packtlib

Do you need instant solutions to your IT questions? PacktLib is Packt's online digital book library. Here, you can search, access, and read Packt's entire library of books.

Why subscribe?

- Fully searchable across every book published by Packt
- Copy and paste, print, and bookmark content
- On demand and accessible via a web browser

Free access for Packt account holders

If you have an account with Packt at www.PacktPub.com, you can use this to access PacktLib today and view 9 entirely free books. Simply use your login credentials for immediate access.

Table of Contents

Preface

Citrix® XenDesktop® is a desktop virtualization and a VDI solution that delivers Windows desktop experience as an on-demand service to any user, anytime, anywhere. It suits all types of workers from task workers and knowledge workers to mobile "work shifting" workers. XenDesktop® delivers complete desktops and applications quickly and in a secure manner while providing a high-definition user experience at the same time.

Instead of managing thousands of static desktop images, you can manage and update the desktop OS and applications once, from a single location. If you can corral all your user resources in the data center, you can get a better grasp of the security and better the policy compliance.

My first book, *Getting Started with XenDesktop® 7.x*, provides comprehensive details on how to design, implement, and maintain a desktop delivery site using XenDesktop®. It teaches you about management, policies, printing, USB support, storage and backup, the **High Definition User Experience (HDX™)**, application delivery, the XenDesktop® SDK, Citrix Receiver™, security, and running XenDesktop® from the cloud.

If you are reading this book, you have most likely implemented XenDesktop® or are sizing and scoping your deployment. Once you have read the first book and understood how to install XenDesktop®, you will want to dig deeper into the topic of optimizing performance. You can't implement XenDesktop® realistically without understanding performance. The more information you have, the more you will be prepared to design and manage performance issues ahead of time.

You may have installed a previous version of XenDesktop® and found that XenDesktop® 7.x is different than the previous versions. This book will be helpful even if you are a desktop virtualization veteran or new to the game and starting fresh. In this book, we will walk through the architecture of Citrix® XenDesktop® to help you understand where the performance weak points are and how to optimize the product.

What this book covers

Chapter 1, XenDesktop® Architecture, covers the definition of some basic XenDesktop® architectures and the different components involved. We learn about some terminologies and concepts that are important to understand as a baseline before addressing performance.

Chapter 2, Sizing, teaches you to size the different components of XenDesktop® architecture. It provides you with some tools to help you keep your deployment within the bounds of comprehension.

Chapter 3, Hypervisors, examines how the virtual hardware operates in general and how it relates to XenDesktop® and then we continue down that path. Before we do that, we need to have a discussion on how virtualization works in relation to the underlying hardware.

Chapter 4, Memory Optimization, covers all of the weak points or places where we might want to focus on optimization, starting with virtual memory.

Chapter 5, Network Optimization, focuses on how the virtual hardware operates in relation to XenDesktop® with regards to networking.

Chapter 6, Storage Optimization, covers arguably the most important and most talked about topic of virtualization. There are many different types of storage, we review them in this chapter and find out which one is best for XenDesktop® and virtualization. It also includes a discussion on the controversial subject of IOPS.

Chapter 7, CPU Optimization, covers CPU virtualization and some concepts around optimizing performance. A lot of information passes through the CPU whether it's virtualized or not. When you install a hypervisor, it carves up the physical CPU into virtual CPUs and with the advent of hyper-threading, the number of vCPUs doubles conceptually.

Chapter 8, Performance Monitoring, focuses on how to monitor the performance of XenDesktop® and includes some sample tools, both GUI and CLI based.

Chapter 9, Acceleration, discusses performance optimization beyond the XenDesktop® site such as the WAN. You can control performance inside the hypervisors, hardware, and datacenter in which you deploy your XenDesktop® infrastructure.

Chapter 10, XenDesktop® Component Tweaks, covers some additional performance-enhancing tweaks for individual VDI components.

What you need for this book

The following are the software components that are required for this book:

- Microsoft Windows Server 2012 R2
- XenDesktop® 7.x
- Citrix® NetScaler®
- Citrix CloudBridge WAN Optimization
- Hypervisor (Citrix® XenServer® 6.x.x, VMware vSphere (ESX 5.x), Microsoft System Center Virtual Machine Manager 2012 Rollup 1 for Hyper-V)

The following are the license requirements for this book:

- Microsoft Windows Server 2012 R2
- Microsoft Windows XP, 7, and 8
- Microsoft Terminal Services
- XenDesktop®
- Citrix® NetScaler®
- Citrix® CloudBridge™ WAN Optimization product

The following are the hardware requirements for this book:

- Hypervisor Host Servers
- Network infrastructure
- Client devices

The following are the XenDesktop® components used in this book:

- StoreFront™
- Delivery Controller
- Studio
- Director
- License Server
- Desktops
- Application Servers
- NetScaler Gateway™:
    - StoreFront™ frontend

- CloudBridge™:
  - ❑ CloudBridge™ Connector
  - ❑ CloudBridge™ WAN Optimization

The following are the Microsoft products used in combination with Citrix® XenDesktop® components that are used in this book:

- Microsoft SQL Server
- Microsoft Active Directory
- Microsoft DHCP
- Microsoft DNS

Who this book is for

If you are a system administrator, architect, consultant, or beginner who has implemented XenDesktop® sites and is looking for tips on performance optimization, then this book is for you. This book will help both new and experienced XenDesktop® professionals to deliver desktops and applications that provide an outstanding user experience.

Conventions

In this book, you will find a number of styles of text that distinguish between different kinds of information. Here are some examples of these styles, and an explanation of their meaning.

Code words in text, database table names, folder names, filenames, file extensions, pathnames, dummy URLs, user input, and Twitter handles are shown as follows:

"You can find out how many are assigned on each XenServer host by running the command `cat /proc/cpuinfo`".

A block of code is set as follows:

```
$grp = Get-XdDesktopGroup 'example'
C:\PS&gt;$grp.Desktops.Add( New-XdVirtualDesktop machine4 )
C:\PS&gt;Set-XdDesktopGroup $grp
```

When we wish to draw your attention to a particular part of a code block, the relevant lines or items are set in bold:

```
$grp = Get-XdDesktopGroup 'example'
C:\PS&gt;$grp.Desktops.Add( New-XdVirtualDesktop machine4 )
C:\PS&gt;Set-XdDesktopGroup $grp
```

Any command-line input or output is written as follows:

```
PS C:\Windows\system32> Set-ExecutionPolicy Unrestricted
```

New terms and **important words** are shown in bold. Words that you see on the screen, in menus or dialog boxes for example, appear in the text like this: "Click on **Advanced** under the properties for TCP/IP version 4".

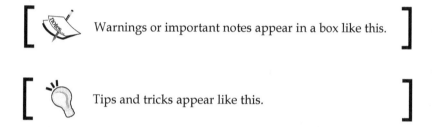

Warnings or important notes appear in a box like this.

Tips and tricks appear like this.

Reader feedback

Feedback from our readers is always welcome. Let us know what you think about this book—what you liked or may have disliked. Reader feedback is important for us to develop titles that you really get the most out of.

To send us general feedback, simply send an e-mail to feedback@packtpub.com, and mention the book title via the subject of your message.

If there is a topic that you have expertise in and you are interested in either writing or contributing to a book, see our author guide on www.packtpub.com/authors.

Customer support

Now that you are the proud owner of a Packt book, we have a number of things to help you to get the most from your purchase.

Downloading the example code

You can download the example code files for all Packt books you have purchased from your account at http://www.packtpub.com. If you purchased this book elsewhere, you can visit http://www.packtpub.com/support and register to have the files e-mailed directly to you.

Downloading the color images of this book

We also provide you with a PDF file that has color images of the screenshots/diagrams used in this book. The color images will help you better understand the changes in the output. You can download this file from: http://www.packtpub.com/sites/default/files/downloads/7688OS_ColorImages.pdf.

Errata

Although we have taken every care to ensure the accuracy of our content, mistakes do happen. If you find a mistake in one of our books—maybe a mistake in the text or the code—we would be grateful if you could report this to us. By doing so, you can save other readers from frustration and help us improve subsequent versions of this book. If you find any errata, please report them by visiting http://www.packtpub.com/submit-errata, selecting your book, clicking on the **Errata Submission Form** link, and entering the details of your errata. Once your errata are verified, your submission will be accepted and the errata will be uploaded to our website or added to any list of existing errata under the Errata section of that title.

To view the previously submitted errata, go to https://www.packtpub.com/books/content/support and enter the name of the book in the search field. The required information will appear under the **Errata** section.

Piracy

Piracy of copyright material on the Internet is an ongoing problem across all media. At Packt, we take the protection of our copyright and licenses very seriously. If you come across any illegal copies of our works, in any form, on the Internet, please provide us with the location address or website name immediately so that we can pursue a remedy.

Please contact us at `copyright@packtpub.com` with a link to the suspected pirated material.

We appreciate your help in protecting our authors, and our ability to bring you valuable content.

Questions

You can contact us at `questions@packtpub.com` if you are having a problem with any aspect of the book, and we will do our best to address it.

1
XenDesktop® Architecture

In this first chapter, we'll start with defining some basic XenDesktop architectures and the different components involved. We'll also visit some terminology and concepts that are important to understand as a baseline before addressing performance. As your XenDesktop sites grow, performance will be impacted, so getting the blueprint right first time is critical. One thing we often say in our business is "measure twice, and cut once". In this chapter, we will cover the following:

- Introduction
- Architecture
- Terminology and concepts
- Components

Introduction

XenDesktop is a desktop virtualization and **Virtual Desktop Infrastructure** (VDI) solution that delivers a Windows desktop experience as an on-demand service to any user, anytime, anywhere. It suits all types of workers, from task workers or knowledge workers, to mobile workshifting workers. XenDesktop quickly and securely delivers complete desktops or applications while providing a high-definition user experience.

XenDesktop is a desktop virtualization solution that optimizes the delivery of desktops, applications, and data to end users. It includes all the capabilities to deliver desktops, applications, and data securely to every type of user in an enterprise. Instead of managing thousands of static desktop images, you can manage and update the desktop OS and applications once, from one location.

My other book, *Getting Started with XenDesktop® 7.x, Packt Publishing*, provides comprehensive details on how to design, implement, and maintain a desktop delivery site using XenDesktop. It also includes topics on management, policies, printing, USB support, storage and backup, the **High Definition User Experience (HDX)**, application delivery, the XenDesktop SDK, the Citrix Receiver, and running XenDesktop from the cloud.

If you are reading this book, you have most likely heard of the desktop virtualization concept. You may have done some basic research on the topic or installed a previous version of XenDesktop. If you are a desktop virtualization veteran or new to the game and starting your proof of concept, this book will be helpful. In this book, we will assume you already have a XenDesktop environment or are planning one. We will help you understand the different topics surrounding XenDesktop performance.

Getting started with hypervisors

Before we get started, you will need to understand what a hypervisor is. A hypervisor is a thin operating system that hosts multiple instances of disparate operating systems. It can also be defined as software that can create and run virtual machines. The hypervisor software runs on server hardware that is enabled for virtualization. Once this is installed, you can install several instances of different operating systems onto the hypervisor. The hypervisor was game-changing, because instead of running one operating system per server, you could now run X number of operating systems on one server, saving space and money.

There are several vendors that make hypervisors, such as Citrix XenServer, VMware ESXi, Microsoft Hyper-V, and the Linux open source **Kernel Virtual Machine (KVM)**. There are two types of hypervisors:

- Type 1 hypervisors, which run directly on the server hardware. These are also known as "bare-metal" hypervisors.
- Type 2 hypervisors, which run on top of an operating system, which then run on the server.

As you can imagine, the Type 1 hypervisors have been touted to have better performance as they interact directly with the server hardware resources.

Citrix XenServer and VMware ESXi are Type 1 hypervisors. Microsoft Hyper-V is presumably a Type 1 hypervisor. There has been debate over whether Hyper-V is a Type 1 or Type 2 hypervisor mainly because you first install the Windows server operating system and then turn on the Hyper-V role, giving the perception that Hyper-V is running on top of or with the help of the Windows Server operating system. Obviously, XenDesktop runs on Citrix XenServer, but it can also run on VMware ESXi and Microsoft Hyper-V.

 At the time of this writing, XenDesktop does not run on KVM. You could probably make it work. Citrix does not officially support KVM. Tribal Knowledge says you could run XenDesktop on KVM, but you would not be able to use MCS or PVS automation for creating VMs.

The following diagram gives you a visual idea of the differences between the types of hypervisors compared to traditional servers. It also shows how the interaction between these components contends for hardware resources and ultimately affects performance and sizing of hardware resources:

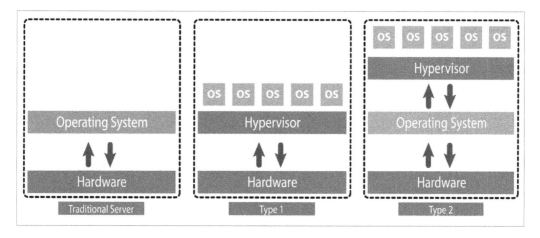

Architecture

Before we can start designing the XenDesktop infrastructure, we need to understand the core components that go into building it. XenDesktop can support all types of workers, from task workers that run Microsoft Office applications, to knowledge users that host business applications, to mobile workshifting users, to high-end 3D application users. XenDesktop scales from a small business supporting five to ten users up to large enterprises supporting thousands of users.

In the XenDesktop architecture, there are several sections called layers that are used to group certain functions together. Each layer is comprised of logical groupings of resources to help you better understand the roles each type of component plays.

The following is a simple diagram to illustrate the components that make up the XenDesktop architecture:

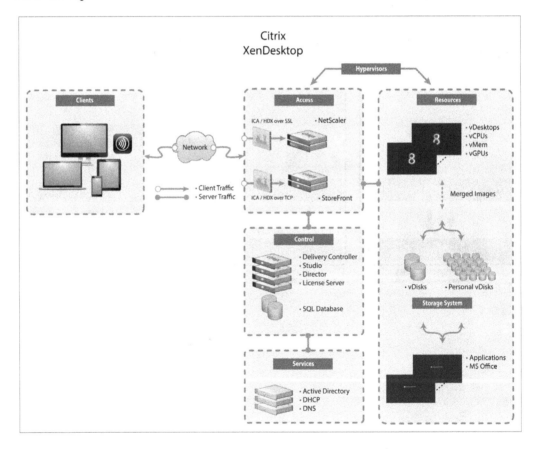

Referring to this diagram, you now have a visual representation of how a simple site will look when finished. Let's take a look at each individual component so you understand the role of each one.

The Clients layer

The **Clients** layer contains all the clients. It seems simple, and it is. Citrix Receiver is device-agnostic, so it will run on any device. You name it, and it will be capable of connecting to a XenDesktop.

The Network layer

One of the benefits of XenDesktop is that it creates a light network load for the client connections. However, we call out the **Network** layer because this is a potential pinch point in large XenDesktop deployments—a place where performance can be degraded or bottlenecked. The network layer is a general term and refers to every piece of the network, from the client device, through the wide area network, the cloud, and into the datacenter where XenDesktop is being hosted.

The Access layer

The **Access** layer is where you place the NetScaler to frontend your XenDesktop site. You can also place the StoreFront servers here. This layer contains resources that provide a portal for your clients to connect to the XenDesktop site. This layer is similar to DMZ computing in traditional network architectures.

Citrix NetScaler provides a SSL encryption frontend for XenDesktop. It is discussed at length in my companion book, *Getting Started with XenDesktop® 7.x, Packt Publishing*.

The Control layer

The **Control** layer contains all the components critical to controlling, managing, monitoring, storing, licensing, and delivering the desktops to the users.

The Services layer

The **Services** layer contains components that are not Citrix products but are essential to the deployment of the XenDesktop site; for example, the Microsoft Active Directory / Domain Controller, DHCP, and DNS.

The Resources layer

The **Resources** layer contains all the XenDesktop consumable resources such as desktops and applications. All the resources to power desktops and applications live here, including vCPUs, vMem, and storage for vDisks and PvDisks.

The Storage System layer

We call out the **Storage System** layer only because storage is increasingly being detached from the servers and could be a pinch point in itself. Conceptually, storage resources could be its own layer.

The Hypervisors layer

The **Hypervisors** layer is not really a layer, but you could refer to it as that. Some abstraction needs to be made regarding the hardware that all this stuff is running on top of. Each layer could conceptually be its own piece of hardware or server with a hypervisor running on top of it, with virtual machines to host XenDesktop components on top of that.

Terminology and concepts

In this section, we will cover some commonly used terminology and concepts used with XenDesktop.

Hyperthreading

Most physical servers designed to be used with a hypervisor include physical CPUs that are capable of hyperthreading. Hyperthreading allows a CPU to be used by more than one process or task at a time. Hyperthreading allows multiple threads to run on each processor core. Simple math would indicate that hyperthreading effectively doubles the CPU count. However, Tribal Knowledge says the extra amount of performance varies, and it is more like a 1.5:1 ratio providing a 20 to 30 percent performance improvement, and not 2:1 with 100 percent performance improvement. A **virtual CPU (vCPU)** or multiple vCPUs are assigned to VMs. Hyperthreading doubles the number of available vCPUs that can be assigned with the caveat mentioned in the preceding section.

The server side

It is important to understand terminology and concepts as they apply to the server side of the XenDesktop architecture. The server side refers to any term, concept, or component to the right of the network cloud.

The client side

The client side refers to any term, concept, or component to the left of the network cloud. To have a complete end-to-end solution, you need to consider an important part of the architecture—the end user device or client. There isn't much to consider here; however, the client devices can range from high-powered Windows desktops to low-end thin clients or mobile devices. There is a software component called Citrix Receiver that is necessary to complete the connection to XenDesktop that runs on the client hardware.

Virtual machine

A virtual machine is a software-implemented version of the hardware.
For example, Windows Server 2012 R2 can be installed as a virtual machine running in XenServer, VMware ESX, and Hyper-V. In fact, every server and desktop in this book's examples can be installed as a VM with the exception of the hypervisor itself, which obviously needs to be installed on the server hardware before we can install any VMs.

 Technically, you could run a hypervisor inside another hypervisor, known as a nested hypervisor, but there is no reason to do this as the performance would not be good.

Server virtual machines

Server VMs are based on a Windows Server operating system used for delivering applications or hosted desktops to users.

Desktop virtual machines

Desktops VMs are based on the Windows desktop operating system used for delivering personalized desktops to users or for delivering applications from desktop operating systems.

XenApp®

Citrix XenApp is an on-demand application delivery solution that enables any Windows application to be virtualized, centralized, and managed in the datacenter and instantly delivered as a service. Prior to XenDesktop 7.x, XenApp delivered applications, server-based and hosted shared desktops (server desktops), and XenDesktop delivered only Windows desktops. Now, with the release of XenDesktop 7.x, it delivers both desktops and applications. XenApp as a standalone product is still available.

EdgeSight®

Citrix EdgeSight is a performance and availability management solution for XenDesktop, XenApp, and endpoint systems. EdgeSight monitors applications, devices, sessions, license usage, and the network in real time. EdgeSight will be phased out as a product, and its functionality will be incorporated into Citrix Director and the HDX Insight Appliance.

FlexCast®

Don't let the term "FlexCast" confuse you. FlexCast is a term designed to encompass all of the different architectures in which XenDesktop can be deployed. FlexCast allows you to deliver virtual desktops and applications according to the needs of diverse performance, security, and flexibility requirements of every type of user in your organization. FlexCast is a way of describing the different ways to deploy XenDesktop. For example, task workers using low-end thin clients at remote offices will use a different FlexCast model than, say, a group of HDX 3D high-end graphics users. The following are the FlexCast models you may want to consider:

FlexCast model	Use case	Citrix products used
Local VM	Local VM desktops extend the benefit of centralized, single-instance management to mobile workers that need to use their laptops offline. Changes to the OS, apps, and data are synchronized when they connect to the network.	XenClient

FlexCast model	Use case	Citrix products used
Streamed VHD	Streamed VHDs leverage the local processing power of rich clients, which provides centralized single-image management of the desktop. This is an easy, low-cost way to get started with desktop virtualization. This is rarely used.	Citrix Receiver XenApp
Hosted VDI	Hosted VDI desktops offer a personalized Windows desktop experience, typically required by office workers, which can be delivered to any device. This combines central management of the desktop with full user personalization. The user's desktop runs in a virtual machine. Users get the same high-definition experience that they had with a local PC, but with centralized management. The VDI approach provides the best combination of security and customization. Personalization is stored in the Personal vDisk. VDI desktops can be accessed from any device such as thin clients, laptops, PCs, and mobile devices. This is the most common model.	Citrix Receiver XenDesktop Personal vDisk
Hosted Shared	Hosted Shared desktops provide a locked down, streamlined, and standardized environment with a core set of applications. This is ideal for task workers where personalization is not required. All the users share a single desktop image. These desktops cannot be modified, except by IT. Hosted Shared desktops are not appropriate for mobile workers or workers that need personalization. They are, however, appropriate for task workers using thin clients.	Citrix Receiver XenDesktop
On-demand applications	On-demand applications allow any Windows application to be centralized and managed in the datacenter, hosted on either multi-user terminal servers or virtual machines and delivered as a service to physical and virtual desktops.	Citrix Receiver XenApp and XenDesktop App Edition

Components

The resource layers in the architecture are a way to group resources according to general functionality. Within each resource layer are specific XenDesktop components. Each component has a function and plays a role in the XenDesktop infrastructure. These components and their roles are discussed in the following section.

Citrix Receiver™

Citrix Receiver is a universal software client that provides secure, high-performance delivery of virtual desktops and applications to any device anywhere. Citrix Receiver is platform-agnostic, meaning that there is a receiver for just about every device out there, from Windows- to Linux-based thin clients to mobile devices including iOS and Android. In fact, some thin client vendors have performed close integration with the Citrix Ready program to embed the Citrix Receiver code directly into their homegrown operating system for seamless operation with XenDesktop.

Citrix Receiver must be installed on the end user client device in order to receive the desktop and applications from XenDesktop. It must also be installed on the virtual desktop in order to receive applications from the application servers (XenApp or XenDesktop), and this is taken care of for you automatically when installing the VDA on the virtual desktop machine.

Citrix Receiver provides users with self-service access to resources published on XenDesktop or XenApp servers. This software combines ease of deployment and uses and offers quick, secure access to hosted applications, desktops, and data.

Hypervisor

A hypervisor is a thin operating system that hosts multiple instances of other operating systems. This concept of one hosting many is the fulcrum of the value of virtualization. XenDesktop is supported on three hypervisors—Citrix XenServer, VMware ESXi, and Microsoft Hyper-V.

NetScaler®

Citrix NetScaler provides the frontend to XenDesktop resources. NetScaler is primarily an **Application Delivery Controller** (**ADC**) that can also perform load balancing. Its primary purpose for XenDesktop, however, is to provide the security for all communications using **Secure Sockets Layer** (**SSL**). Think of it this way: for those organizations that want to secure their communications, traffic comes into the NetScaler using encrypted SSL. You can choose not to use SSL, but it is not recommended.

StoreFront™

Citrix StoreFront is the portal that authenticates users to site(s) hosting XenDesktop resources and manages stores of desktops and applications that users access. Active Directory does the actual authentication and interacts with StoreFront.

 StoreFront replaces Web Interface from previous versions.

Delivery Controller

The Citrix Delivery Controller brokers access to desktops and applications and manages user access. Each site has one or more Delivery Controllers.

Studio

Citrix Studio is the management console that enables you to configure and manage your XenDesktop and XenApp deployment, eliminating the need for two separate management consoles for managing the delivery of desktops and applications.

 If you use provisioning services, also included in XenDesktop, then you need to use the provisioning server console to deploy the VMs on the hosting platform.

Studio provides various wizards to guide you through the process of setting up your environment, creating your workloads to host and assign applications and desktops, and assigning applications and desktops to users.

 Citrix Studio replaces the delivery services console and Citrix app center from previous XenDesktop versions. Studio is used to configure the XenDesktop site.

Director

Citrix Director is used to monitor and troubleshoot XenDesktop deployment.

 Director is the console that is used to monitor and manage the sessions.

The License Server

The Citrix License Server serves licenses. Every Citrix product and every XenDesktop user requires a Citrix license. Studio consults the License Server to check out and check in licenses.

The only exception is NetScaler, which is licensed from within NetScaler itself.

Database

In XenDesktop, we use Microsoft SQL Server. The database is sometimes referred to as the data store. Almost everything in XenDesktop is database driven and the SQL database holds all state information, in addition to session and configuration information.

If the database server fails, existing connections to virtual desktops will continue to function until the user either logs off or disconnects from their virtual desktop. In XenDesktop version 7.6, Citrix introduced the Connection Leasing feature, which allows new connections to occur even if the database is unavailable. Citrix recommends you to implement SQL mirroring and clustering for high availability.

> The IMA data store is no longer used, and everything is now done in the SQL database for both session and configuration information. The data collector is shared evenly across XenDesktop controllers.

Active Directory

Microsoft Active Directory is required for authentication and authorization. Active Directory can also be used for controller discovery by desktops to discover the controllers within a site. Desktops determine which controllers are available by referring to information that controllers publish in Active Directory.

> If you don't want to use Active Directory for authentication, you can create an anonymous store in StoreFront and use local authentication.

Active Directory's built-in security infrastructure is used by desktops to verify that communications between controllers come from authorized controllers on the appropriate site. Active Directory's security infrastructure also ensures that the data exchanged by desktops and controllers is confidential.

 Installing XenDesktop on the domain controller is not supported; in fact, it is not even possible.

DHCP

Every machine in this architecture—virtual or physical, client, desktop, or server—requires an IP address. XenDesktop uses the Microsoft DHCP service to centrally manage IP addresses.

DNS

Every machine and service in XenDesktop needs a way to convert **Fully Qualified Domain Names (FQDNs)** into IP addresses so they can send packets out on the network and reach their destination. XenDesktop uses the Microsoft DNS service to do this.

 You can also use the **Berkeley Internet Name Domain (BIND)** server.

Desktop

A desktop is the instantiation of a complete Windows operating system, typically Windows XP, 7, or 8. In XenDesktop, we create the desktop VM and add the VDA to it so that it can work with XenDesktop and be delivered to clients. This will become the end user's virtual desktop.

 At the time of this writing, XenDesktop 7.x does not support Windows 10.

Server

A server is a virtual machine dedicated to performing one or more specific tasks on the XenDesktop site, for example, brokering connections (Delivery Controller). These virtual machines can be used to host applications. More importantly, these servers are used to host the important XenDesktop components such as StoreFront, Delivery Controller, Studio, Director, License Server, SQL Server, Active Directory, DHCP, and DNS.

Storage

All the XenDesktop components use storage. There are two types of storage in this architecture. First, there is SQL Server, which is used as the database for the XenDesktop components. Then, there are **Virtual Disks (vDisks)** and **Personal Virtual Disks (PvDisks)**.

vDisk

In a dedicated model, each user gets their own vDisk, which hosts the desktop OS. As you can imagine, the storage requirements for a dedicated vDisk model can grow quite substantially. In a pooled/shared model, several users share the same vDisk. There are other types of vDisk deployment models. The different types of vDisks are explained in the following table:

vDisk model	Description	Performance impact
Static vs. random	A static desktop is assigned to a specific user. Each time that user logs on, they get the same desktop they had before. A random desktop is just that; the user will likely get a different desktop than they had before.	Static desktops are faster than random desktops.
Pooled vs. assigned	The pooled desktops (random) are just that; shared resources maintained in a pool and shared across many users. An assigned desktop (static) is a desktop that is assigned to a specific user and only that user.	An assigned desktop is faster than a pooled desktop.
Persistent vs. non-persistent	A persistent desktop (static, assigned) is a desktop that retains its state and settings when the user logs out. A non-persistent desktop (random, pooled) doesn't keep its state when the user logs out, and it is returned to the pool for a different user to use.	Persistent desktops are faster than non-persistent desktops.

Personal vDisk

The concept of the PvDisk is powerful for the users. PvDisk provides a personalization feature for storing personal data from virtual desktops. Each user gets their own Personal vDisk that stores their user profile, data, and applications that are unique to them. They are smaller than OS vDisks. They allow you to scale by pooling and sharing vDisks among many users and giving them each their own smaller Personal vDisk. PvDisks are merged with vDisks at runtime—the appearance to the end user is seamless.

 Using a pooled / shared vDisk model in combination with PvDisks is most scalable and practical. However, PvDisks use more IOPS, so it may affect performance.

Virtual Desktop Agent

The **Virtual Desktop Agent (VDA)** has to be installed on the virtual machine to which users will be connecting. It enables the machines to register with controllers and manages the connection between the machines and the user devices. The VDA is installed on the operating system VM, such as Windows XP, 7, or 8, which gets served to the client. The VDA maintains a heartbeat with the Delivery Controller, updates policies, and registers with the Delivery Controller.

Summary

You now have a good grasp of the logical grouping of XenDesktop components and the terminology used in XenDesktop. This chapter also serves as a good reference to look back on as you move forward.

You now know what a XenDesktop site will look like from the network diagram, components, terminology, and concepts. In the next chapter, we'll look at system requirements for XenDesktop components, compatible hypervisor hosts, and the most important topic of the sizing. Using the sizing techniques and calculations in the next chapter will give you a solid blueprint for your VDI deployment from small to extra large XenDesktop sites.

2
Sizing

In the first chapter, we started with defining some basic XenDesktop architectures, terminology, concepts, and components. Now, we'll learn how to size them. While none of the XenDesktop site is the same, you need to start somewhere. That somewhere is here, where we give you some tools to help you keep your deployment within the bounds of comprehension. Sizing the environment is critical to understanding where the different components will be placed and how to prepare to build them. As your site grows, performance will be impacted if it isn't designed well, so getting the blueprint right the first time is critical. One thing we often say in our business is measure twice, and cut once. What that means is do your planning and scoping in great analysis, and do it more than once before you start ordering and deploying. In this chapter, we will cover the following:

- System requirements
- Hypervisor hosts
- XenDesktop sizing

 Tribal Knowledge indicates you should size for "peak" usage, boot storms, logon storms, and resource hungry users. Otherwise, users will be disappointed.

System requirements

Each component has its requirements in terms of the operating system and licensing. You will need to build these operating systems on **virtual machines** (**VMs**) before installing each component. For help with creating VMs, look at the relevant hypervisor documentation.

Citrix Receiver™

Citrix Receiver is a universal software client that provides secure, high-performance delivery of virtual desktops and applications. Citrix Receiver is available for Windows, Mac, the mobile devices iOS and Android, HTML5, Chromebook, and Java 10.1.

You will need to install Citrix Receiver once for a complete end-to-end connection to be made to the desktop, and again on the VDA if you want access to published applications.

Once on the end user's client device, there are many supported devices including iOS and Android, and you will also need to install Citrix Receiver for Windows on the Windows virtual desktop that you will serve up to your users if they require access to published applications (optional). This is done automatically while installing the **Virtual Desktop Agent** (**VDA**) on the Windows virtual desktop.

You will need the Citrix Receiver to access the applications that are running on a separate application server (XenApp or XenDesktop). If you provide complete virtual desktops with App-V applications and no additional published applications are needed, then you would not need to install Citrix Receiver on the virtual desktop.

StoreFront 3.x

StoreFront replaces the web interface. StoreFront 3.x can also be used with XenApp and XenDesktop 5.5 and above. The supported operating systems are as follows:

- Windows Server 2012 R2, Standard or Datacenter
- Windows Server 2012, Standard or Datacenter
- Windows Server 2008 R2 SP1, Standard or Enterprise

The system requirements are as follows:

- RAM: 4 GB + 8 MB per 1000 users
- Microsoft **Internet Information Services** (**IIS**)
- Microsoft Internet Information Services Manager
- .NET Framework 4.0
- Firewall ports–external: As StoreFront is the gateway to the site, you will need to open specific ports on the firewall to allow connections in ports 80 (http) and 443 (https)
- Firewall ports–internal: By default, StoreFront communicates with the internal XenDesktop Delivery Controller servers using the ports 80 (for StoreFront servers) and 8080 (for HTML5 clients)

You can specify different ports, too.

 For more information on StoreFront and how to plug it into the architecture, refer to `http://bit.ly/xen-sf`.

Database–Microsoft SQL Server

If you recall, we talked about the database in *Chapter 1, XenDesktop® Architecture*. Almost everything in XenDesktop is database driven and the SQL database holds all the state information, in addition to session and configuration information. The supported Microsoft SQL Server versions are as follows:

- SQL Server 2014: Express, Standard, and Enterprise Edition
- SQL Server 2012 SP1: Express, Standard, and Enterprise Edition
- SQL Server 2008 R2 SP2: Express, Standard, Enterprise, and Datacenter Edition

 The installer deploys SQL Express automatically. It can also be found on the XenDesktop installation media in the `Support` folder.

 SQL Express should never be used in production.

The following databases are also supported:

- SQL Server clustered instances
- SQL Server mirroring
- SQL Server 2012 AlwaysOn Availability Groups

Studio

Studio is the management console that enables you to configure and manage your XenDesktop and XenApp deployment. The supported operating systems are as follows:

- Windows 8.1: Pro and Enterprise
- Windows 8: Pro and Enterprise

- Windows 7: Pro, Enterprise, and Ultimate
- Windows Server 2012 R2: Standard and Datacenter
- Windows Server 2012: Standard and Datacenter
- Windows Server 2008 R2 SP1: Standard, Enterprise, and Datacenter

The system requirements are as follows:

- 75 MB disk space
- Microsoft .NET Framework 3.5 SP1 (Windows 2008 R2 only)
- Microsoft Management Console 3.0
- Windows PowerShell 2.0 (Windows 7 and Windows 2008 R2) or PowerShell 3.0 (Windows 8.1, Windows 8, Windows 2012 R2, and Windows 2012)

 MMC 3.0 and PowerShell are included with Windows Server.

The Delivery Controller

The Delivery Controller brokers access to desktops and applications and manages user access. Each XenDesktop site can have one or more Delivery Controllers. The supported operating systems are as follows:

- Windows Server 2012 R2: Standard or Datacenter Edition
- Windows Server 2012: Standard or Datacenter Edition
- Windows Server 2008 R2: Standard or Enterprise Edition

The system requirements are as follows:

- 100 MB disk space
- Microsoft .NET Framework 3.5 SP1 (Windows 2008 R2 only)
- Microsoft .NET 4.0
- Windows PowerShell 2.0 (included with Windows 2008 R2) or PowerShell 3.0 (included with Windows 2012 R2)
- Visual C++ 2005, 2008 SP1, and 2010 Redistributable Package

The installer installs the software described in the previous section for you automatically. It is also available on the XenDesktop installation media in the Support folder.

Director

Director is used to manage, monitor, and troubleshoot the XenDesktop site with a specific focus on user sessions, shadowing, HDX, and so on. The supported operating systems are as follows:

- Windows Server 2012 R2: Standard or Datacenter
- Windows Server 2012: Standard or Datacenter
- Windows Server 2008 R2 SP1: Standard or Datacenter

The system requirements are as follows:

- 50 MB disk space
- Microsoft .NET Framework 4.0

 The installer deploys this automatically for you.

- Microsoft Internet Information Services 7.0 and ASP.NET 2.0

The supported browsers for viewing Director are as follows:

- Internet Explorer 11, 10, and 9 (IE 10 compatibility mode is not supported)
- Firefox
- Chrome

License Server 11.x

The License Server stores and manages licenses for the Citrix products.

The supported operating systems are as follows:

- Windows Server 2012 R2: Standard or Datacenter
- Windows Server 2012: Standard or Datacenter
- Windows Server 2008 R2 SP1: Standard or Enterprise

The system requirements are as follows:

- 3 GB RAM
- .NET Framework 3.5 SP1 or greater

NetScaler VPX™

The Citrix NetScaler VPX is a virtual machine instantiation of the appliance-based NetScaler.

The supported hypervisors are as follows:

- Citrix XenServer
- VMware vSphere 5.x
- Microsoft Hyper-V (SCVMM)

The minimum system requirements are as follows:

- 3 GB RAM
- 40 GB disk space

 The Citrix NetScaler comes in hardware versions, as well—the MPX and SDX models. The hardware version provides higher performance, so you should consider this in large deployments.

CloudBridge VPX™ (WAN Optimization)

The Citrix CloudBridge VPX is a virtual machine instantiation of the appliance-based CloudBridge.

The supported hypervisors are as follows:

- Citrix XenServer
- VMware vSphere 5.x
- Microsoft Hyper-V (SCVMM)

The minimum system requirements are as follows:

- 2 GB RAM
- 100 GB disk space

The CloudBridge product is not a requirement for XenDesktop, but it can be useful in accelerating high latency connections. There are hardware versions available as well.

Virtual Delivery Agent

The VDA is also referred to as the **Delivery Agent** (**DA**) in the book. It is available for both Windows desktop OSs as well as Windows Server OSs. The VDA is installed on Windows desktops and on Windows application servers.

The supported operating systems are as follows:

- Windows 8.1: Pro or Enterprise
- Windows 8: Pro or Enterprise
- Windows 7 SP1: Pro, Enterprise, or Ultimate
- Windows Server 2008 R2 SP1: Datacenter, Enterprise, or Standard
- Windows Server 2012 R2: Standard or Datacenter
- Windows Server 2012: Standard or Datacenter
- Windows Server 2008 R2 SP1: Standard, Enterprise, or Datacenter

The installer automatically deploys the necessary components such as the Microsoft .NET Framework and the Visual C++ Runtime Library. The Visual C++ components are also available on the XenDesktop installation media in the Support folder.

Multimedia acceleration features for HDX require Microsoft Media Foundation to be installed prior to installing the VDA on the machine.

 To use a Windows XP or Vista machine with XenDesktop 7.x, you will need to install an earlier version of the Citrix VDA, which can be downloaded from the https://www.citrix.com/ website.

Microsoft Active Directory

XenDesktop is integrated tightly with Microsoft Active Directory. XenDesktop uses Active Directory for user authentication and authorization. It is also integrated with the policies in Active Directory.

Citrix policies, in Active Directory, control users in their connections, security, bandwidth usage, drive mapping, local access, and so on. The supported operating system is as follows:

- Windows Server 2003 or higher

Microsoft DHCP Server

All your XenDesktop component servers should have static IP addresses. DHCP is used to hand out IP addresses to the desktops. If you have 100 or more desktops, this is the only way to do it. The supported operating system is as follows:

- Windows Server 2003 or higher

 Tribal Knowledge says that you can use any DHCP server as long as it complies with RFC 2131; Microsoft DHCP is not a hard requirement. Also, if you use IPv6, you don't need to use static IP addresses.

Microsoft DNS Server

DNS resolves **Fully Qualified Domain Names (FQDN)** to IP addresses. XenDesktop uses standard computer object attributes in Active Directory to manage desktops. Depending on your setup, the machine objects and FQDN are stored in Active Directory and returned to a user when they make a connection. Client machine names are stored in DNS. Connection information and DNS information are kept in sync. The supported operating system is as follows:

- Windows Server 2003 or higher

Tribal Knowledge says you can use any DNS server; Microsoft DNS is not a hard requirement.

Hypervisor host

The hypervisor is a thin operating system that sits between the hardware and the virtual machines.

XenDesktop is virtualization software, but it has to run on something. That something is hypervisor software.

Tribal Knowledge says that you can run XenDesktop on physical hardware without any hypervisor; however, there aren't many use cases for this.

For reference, in a Type-1 hypervisor deployment, XenDesktop runs on top of an operating system, which runs on top of a hypervisor, which runs on top of the server physical hardware.

The supported hypervisor operating systems are as follows:

- Citrix XenServer 6.0.2, 6.1, 6.2, and 6.5
- VMware ESXi 5.0 update 2, vSphere 5.1 update 1, and vSphere 5.5 update 2
- Microsoft Hyper-V 2012 R2, 2012 SP1, or 2012

To see a list of server hardware that is compatible with the hypervisor you choose, search for a hardware compatibility list for hypervisor on the Internet, or go to the following links:

- XenServer HCL: `http://bit.ly/hcl-xen`
- VMware ESXi HCL: `http://bit.ly/hcl-vmware`
- Hyper-V HCL: `http://bit.ly/hcl-hv`

A more exhaustive list of supported hypervisors can be found at `http://bit.ly/hcl-all`.

XenDesktop® site sizing calculations

Now that you understand XenDesktop architectures, terminology, concepts, components, system requirements, and hypervisors, it's time to size up your installation. Sizing is a critical first step in your design because it will generate a blueprint on how much and how big your infrastructure will need to be. Don't worry; it's not rocket science. We start with simple principles of small, medium, large, and beyond while using basic math.

You start out with something that you know, which is the number of users you plan to serve desktops to. You can then determine which category your deployment will fall into, such as small, medium, large, or beyond.

All of the calculations given in the following table and in the accompanying sizing spreadsheet have hypervisor "overhead" capacity built in.

The following table explains the variables used in the calculations described in the preceding section:

Variable	Description
vCPUs	This is the number of virtual CPUs assigned to a user
vUsers	This is the number of virtual desktops deployed to users
vMem	This is the amount of RAM allocated to each desktop
WCache	This is the size of the write cache
Storage capacity	This is the total capacity of the storage device
vDisk	This is the amount of disk space allocated to the master OS
PvDisk	This is the amount of Personal vDisk space allocated to each user for personal storage
numvDisks	This is the number of vDisks to be shared
vRAMHeadroom	This is the amount of extra RAM needed for hypervisor and virtual machine processing
vDiskHeadroom	This is the amount of extra disk space needed for hypervisor and virtual machine processing
HypervisorCPU	The hypervisor typically requires its own CPU for processing
AVMon	The CPUs incur overhead with AntiVirus installed and when using monitoring tools
PvDiskHeadroom	The CPUs incur additional overhead when using Personal vDisk

Storage calculation

The amount of storage needed to support your XenDesktop site can be reduced to a mathematical equation. The preferred way to scale is to use Personal vDisks, so you will likely choose that formula and not the host-dedicated formula. The only time you would use both of the following formulas together is when you have a mix of pooled disk users and dedicated disk users:

Pooled Desktop Storage = (((vUsers * PvDisk) + (vUsers * (vMem + WCache)) * (1+vRAMHeadroom)) + (vUsers * vDisk / numvDisks)) * (1+vDiskHeadroom)

Hosted Dedicated Desktop Storage = ((vUsers * (vDisk + PvDisk)) + (vUsers * (vMem + WCache)) * (1+vRAMHeadroom)) * (1+vDiskHeadroom)

Total Estimated Storage = Pooled Storage + Dedicated Storage

vMem–memory calculation

The amount of RAM needed to support your XenDesktop site can be reduced to a mathematical equation:

*RAM (GB) = (Amount of RAM per desktop * Number of desktops or users) + Hypervisor overhead*

vCPU–CPU calculation

The number of **virtual CPUs (vCPUs)** can be calculated as well. Increasing the number of motherboard CPU sockets does not linearly increase the user count. Multiple users can be serviced from a single CPU. And now that most server vendors offer chipsets that perform hyperthreading, you can really get user density packed into a single server:

*vCPUs = Number of users (desktops) * Number of vCPUs / Number of Users per core + Hypervisor CPU + AntiVirus Overhead + Personal vDisk Overhead*

vNIC–network bandwidth

The amount of network bandwidth each virtual machine will use is calculated by the following formula:

vNIC = Amount of network bandwidth used in Gbps

User type

Not all users are created equal. Depending on the type of users you have, the requirements change ever so slightly. You could have light users who do basic office tasks, or heavy users who do heavy computations and use demanding applications:

The following table illustrates the impact user types have on sizing:

User group	OS	vCPU per desktop	RAM per desktop (GB)	Avg IOPS per desktop	Users per core (CPU)	Estimated storage (GB)
Light	Win XP	1	1	5	12	5
	Win 7, 8	1	2	10	10	20
Normal	Win XP	1	2	10	10	5

User group	OS	vCPU per desktop	RAM per desktop (GB)	Avg IOPS per desktop	Users per core (CPU)	Estimated storage (GB)
	Win 7, 8	2	2	20	8	20
Power	Win XP	1	2	16	8	5
	Win 7, 8	2	3	40	6	20
Heavy	Win XP	1	2	25	6	5
	Win 7, 8	2	4	50	4	20

For a small proof of concept sites, all server roles (virtual machines) can be placed on one physical server. However, as you might have guessed by the network diagram, it's not that simple in a real life production system, especially when you need to plan for growth and scalability. You will need to choose a small, medium, large, or beyond XenDesktop site and start building toward that. Taking the information from the preceding table, we can calculate the amount of memory, CPU, and storage we will need for each type of deployment.

Small XenDesktop® site

A small XenDesktop site is defined as one with 100 users or less. For a small XenDesktop site with 100 users running Windows 8 desktops and pooled storage with Personal vDisks, you get the following:

User type	Users	Total RAM (GB)	Total vCPUs	Total storage (GB)	Total number of servers
Light	100	250	11	2,036	1
Normal	100	250	26	2,036	1
Power	100	375	34	2,180	1
Heavy	100	500	51	2,324	1

Tribal Knowledge says you should never perform a single server deployment for a production system.

Keep in mind that when you go to buy servers, they are usually bound by one of three things: memory, CPU, or storage. The types of servers and associated memory, CPU, and storage in the marketplace vary widely, so you will need to find servers that fit into your calculations. As of this writing, the limiting factor out of the three is vCPUs or processor cores. You can find servers with plenty of memory and storage that are external. The expensive part–vCPU–will be limited to the number you can have in one physical server.

Medium XenDesktop® site

A medium size XenDesktop site is defined as one with 1,000 users or less. For a medium XenDesktop site with 1,000 users running Windows 8 desktops and pooled storage with Personal vDisks, you get the following:

User type	Users	Total RAM (GB)	Total vCPUs	Total storage (GB)	Total number of servers
Light	1,000	2,500	101	21,083	2
Normal	1,000	2,500	251	21,083	4
Power	1,000	3,750	334	22,521	6
Heavy	1,000	5,000	501	23,958	8

Large XenDesktop® site

A large XenDesktop site is defined as one with 5,000 users or less. For a large XenDesktop site with 5,000 users running Windows 8 desktops and pooled storage with Personal vDisks, you get the following:

User type	Users	Total RAM (GB)	Total vCPUs	Total storage (GB)	Total number of servers
Light	5,000	12,500	501	119,792	8
Normal	5,000	12,500	1,251	11,9792	20

User type	Users	Total RAM (GB)	Total vCPUs	Total storage (GB)	Total number of servers
Power	5,000	18,750	1,668	126,979	27
Heavy	5,000	25,000	2,501	134,167	40

Enterprise XenDesktop® site

An Enterprise XenDesktop site or beyond large, XenDesktop site, is defined as on having 5,000 users ore more. In our calculations, we use 10,000 as a good round number. For a beyond large Enterpise XenDesktop site with 10,000 users running Windows 8 desktops and pooled storage with Personal vDisks, you get the following:

User type	Users	Total RAM (GB)	Total vCPUs	Total storage (GB)	Total number of servers
Light	10,000	25,000	1,001	268,333	16
Normal	10,000	25,000	2,501	268,333	40
Power	10,000	37,500	3,334	282,708	53
Heavy	10,000	50,000	5,001	297,083	79

An exhaustive spreadsheet has been built for these calculations, and I've made it available for your use at http://bit.ly/xdp-sizing2.

Some assumptions should be put forth regarding the sizing tool. It assumes that **Machine Creation Services** (**MCS**) is used as opposed to **Provisioning Services** (**PVS**). PVS is being phased out, while MCS is being phased in as a product. However, Tribal Knowledge says that PVS gives you much greater performance. PVS is more complex to use than MCS. The tool doesn't take into account mixed Flexcast models where pooled desktops are combined with static desktops, and it is assumed that Personal vDisk is used. The tool would need to be modified to account for these scenarios.

Some useful tips are as follows:

- Additional calculations can be found in the Citrix Virtual Desktop Handbook for XenDesktop 7.x, which can be found at `http://bit.ly/XD7xdh`

- Remember to use the Internet to search for XenDesktop sizing guides and best practices, and don't forget to try out the Citrix Project Accelerator at `http://project.citrix.com`

- Make sure you download the sizing spreadsheet for all the detailed calculations you will need for appropriate sizing

- There is a fairly well-written test guide that contains parameters and sizing for a 5,000 user deployment, and it can be found at `http://bit.ly/xdp-5000users`

Summary

You are now armed with the information from *Chapter 1, XenDesktop® Architecture,* plus a deeper knowledge of system requirements and how to perform a sizing exercise used in XenDesktop. This chapter also serves as a good reference to look back on as you move forward.

3
Hypervisors

You've learned about XenDesktop architectures, terminology, concepts, components, and sizing. Examining how the virtual hardware operates in general and how it relates to XenDesktop is key, and we will continue down that path. Before we do that, however, we need to have a discussion on how virtualization works in relation to the underlying hardware. In this chapter, we will cover the following topics:

- VMware rings
- XenServer domains
- Hyper-V partitions
- Full virtualization
- Paravirtualization
- XenServer Tools
- VMware Tools
- Hyper-V Tools

VMware rings

Hardware virtualization is a challenge. Each hypervisor has its own internal structure and resources for handling it. Without these things, each virtual machine would suffer terribly with regard to performance. VMware ESXi uses the concept of rings. They refer to the rings as rings of privilege.

- Ring 0 is reserved for the ESXi hypervisor operating system and has the highest privilege. The hypervisor reserves this so that it can have direct access to the physical hardware. The hypervisor kernel running in Ring 0 creates and manages virtual machines and hardware resources. In terms of server architecture, this is similar to kernel space. So, for the most part, the ESXi hypervisor runs in Ring 0.

- Rings 1-3 are where the virtual machines run. In terms of server architecture, this is similar to user space. Your virtual machines and applications run in the higher level rings. You can have multiple higher level rings running on top of Ring 0.

The following diagram shows the structure of rings:

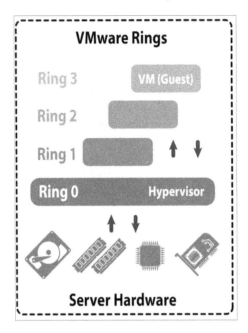

XenServer® domains

XenServer, which is built on open source Xen, takes a slightly different approach. Recognizing the need for different layers that need different privileges for accessing the underlying resources, XenServer uses the concept of Dom0 and DomU, and with the release of XenServer v6.5, Dom0 is now a 64-bit architecture. The following is a detailed description of them:

- **Dom0** stands for **Domain 0** and is the privileged space that provides access to disks, networks, memory, and CPUs. Dom0 contains all the necessary drivers to provide access to the virtual machines. Dom0 is similar to kernel space.

- Virtual machines and applications run in **DomU**, which stands for **Domain User** or **User Domain**. Providing access to the underlying hardware in Xen is done through backend drivers in Dom0 that communicate with frontend drivers in DomU. DomU is where your virtual machines run. In terms of server architectures, DomU is analogous to user space. You can have multiple DomUs running on top of Dom0:

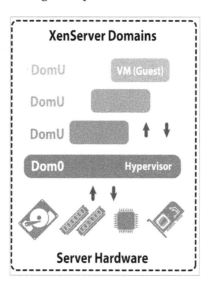

Hyper-V partitions

Microsoft's Hyper-V hypervisor uses the concept of partitions. This is how it provides separation between the hypervisor required privileged access to the underlying hardware and the virtual machines that need to take advantage of that access. The following are the two types of partition:

- The **root partition**, or **parent partition**, has the ability to provide direct access to the underlying hardware. The hypervisor runs in the root partition (Windows server). The root partition is equivalent to the kernel space.

- **Child partitions** have lower privileges and run the virtual machines, and you can have many child partitions running on top of the parent partition. The virtual machines and applications run in the child partitions. Requests from virtual machines to physical devices are redirected through the hypervisor running in the parent or root partition to the physical devices. The child partition is analogous to the user space:

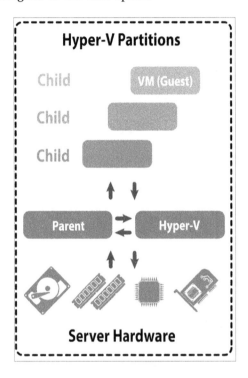

Full virtualization

Full virtualization (FV) is a complete virtual emulation of the physical hardware where every feature and function of the physical hardware is made available to virtual machines including interrupts, memory access, network functions, storage, CPUs, and instruction sets.

Full virtualization was initially attractive and useful because you could run any operating system as a virtual machine. The downside is that it is very slow because the hypervisor must emulate all the physical devices in the server in order to run the VM. Some hypervisors, like XenServer, automatically turn on paravirtualization drivers when running machines in full virtualization.

In full virtualization, the underlying hardware is emulated by the hypervisor. The virtual machine is unaware of the hypervisor and the simulation taking place. For this reason, full virtualization virtual machines can be slow.

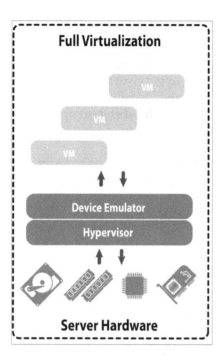

Paravirtualization

Paravirtualization (PV) is a technique used in virtualization that presents a software interface to virtual machines that represents the underlying hardware. Essentially, it means that virtual machines will see and use the underlying hardware just as they normally would if they were running as a single operating system on a physical server. The virtual machine has been modified or enhanced to work with the hypervisor through an API, for example. This is where XenTools and VMware Tools come into play, and we will talk about that more later.

 In paravirtualization, the virtual machine and the hypervisor know about each other and work together. Paravirtualization is optimized and fast.

PV abstracts the underlying hardware into software-based hardware constructs. Paravirtualization was first introduced by the Xen hypervisor team. The first time I came across the concept of paravirtualization was when I was working on marrying the first open source router (Vyatta) with the Xen hypervisor. The CTO at the time said "make sure you are using the paravirtualization drivers to get the best performance". This was questionable then, as not all vendors supported PV yet. In paravirtualization, a virtual machine makes a system call to the hypervisor, and the hypervisor puts the virtual machine in touch with the hardware. In paravirtualization, the virtual machines (guest) drivers are hypervisor-aware, and they work with the hypervisor to integrate closely with hardware resources. Paravirtualization provides high performance. All hypervisors have paravirtualization drivers available for different operating systems such as the Windows and Linux servers, and so on:

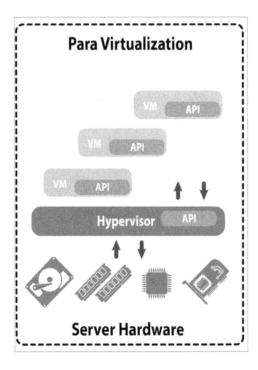

 XenServer touts paravirtualization as their leading differentiator for performance gains.

Hardware-assisted virtualization

Hardware-assisted virtualization (**HAV**) is only possible with hardware, hypervisors, and operating systems that support it. In the mid 2000s, both Intel and AMD came out with their hardware extensions to specifically support virtualization in the form of the AMD-V and Intel VT-x extensions. Most servers support these vendor extensions today, but they need to be enabled or turned on in the BIOS of the server.

As the hardware vendors AMD and Intel make more gains in developing their hardware to interoperate better with virtualization, the HAV model will continue to make gains in performance. One example of how this is done is by taking privileged CPU instructions to automatically trap the hypervisor and run them in what is called the **root mode privilege level**. Also, the virtual machine state can be stored within structures inside the Intel VT-X or AMD-V structures.

Advances in the form of hardware-assisted virtualization by vendors such as Intel and AMD are making HAV quite usable in terms of performance:

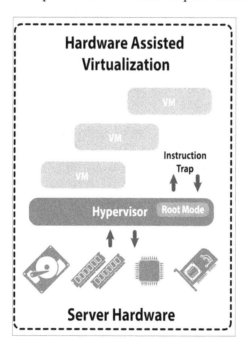

Hypervisor Tools

So, why are we even discussing all this? We are discussing this because all the XenDesktop servers, desktops, and applications run inside virtual machines on the hypervisor host. How those virtual machines cooperate with the hypervisor affects performance. The hypervisor you choose, whether it be VMware ESXi, Citrix XenServer, or Microsoft Hyper-V, will affect the performance of your XenDesktop site. As it turns out, paravirtualization techniques provide the best performance to date. In order to take advantage of the high performance features, hypervisors need to install drivers into the virtual machine. These come in the form of "tools" specific to the hypervisor itself. Along with performance features, these tools also provide enhanced manageability.

VMware Tools

VMware Tools is a suite of utilities that enhances the performance of the virtual machine's operating system and improves the manageability of the virtual machine. Without it installed, the virtual machine will lose functionality and suffer in performance.

VMware Tools does a number of things, but the most important thing is that it provides an API-like interface between the virtual machine and the hypervisor paravirtualization. In a XenDesktop environment, you would be crazy to leave these tools uninstalled as you won't get good performance without them.

The VMware Tools service provides a backdoor to the **virtual machine monitor** (**VMM**), which is part of the hypervisor. The VMM in the VMware hypervisor is used for services such as time synchronization, logging, and guest shutdown. Vmxnet and Vmxnet3 are paravirtualized I/O device drivers that share data structures with the hypervisor. They take advantage of host device capabilities to offer improved throughput and reduced CPU utilization. It is important to note that the VMware Tools service and Vmxnet device drivers are not CPU paravirtualization solutions. They are minimal, non-intrusive changes installed into the guest OS that do not require OS kernel modification. VMware produces these tools for every kind of operating system, including Microsoft Windows.

 There is a good VMware knowledge base article available at `http://kb.vmware.com/kb/340`.

Installing VMware Tools provides a virtual machine with the following:

- Better video resolution
- Better color depth
- Better mouse integration and operability
- Better copy, paste, and drag-and-drop capability
- Better sound
- Quiesced snapshots of the virtual machine
- Synchronized time
- High performance drivers
- Support for hypervisor to virtual machine API calls

If you are using VMware as your hypervisor, you should install VMware Tools onto all the virtual machines in the XenDesktop architecture.

VMware Tools can be installed on Windows from `http://kb.vmware.com/kb/1018377.`

If you are installing VMware Tools on a number of Windows virtual machines, you can automate its installation when using vCenter server by selecting the **Virtual Machines** tab for a host or cluster and then selecting the virtual machines on which to install or upgrade VMware Tools.

To install VMware Tools on vSphere visit `http://kb.vmware.com/kb/2004754.`

XenServer® Tools

XenServer Tools provide high performance Windows drivers and a management agent that enhances performance between the XenDesktop. The paravirtualization drivers in XenServer enable Windows running in the user space DomU to access the resources in the hypervisor kernel space, or Dom0.

Initially, Citrix systems produced paravirtualized drivers for Windows as part of their commercial XenServer virtualization suite. Now, these drivers are available as a standard distribution with the XenServer hypervisor, as a result of Citrix recently submitting the XenServer project to the Apache Open Source Foundation. Advanced features of XenServer and XenCenter require purchase of the commercial version from Citrix.

You could conceptually run Windows virtual machines in open source Xen. Before Citrix submitted the XenServer product back into the open source community through the Apache foundation, it lacked PV drivers for Windows, and performance would therefore suffer greatly. Today, the PV drivers are available in the open source Xen hypervisor as well as the commercial XenServer hypervisor.

Installing XenServer Tools provides the virtual machine with the following:

- The ability to quickly and cleanly shut down, reboot, or suspend a virtual machine
- Migration using XenMotion
- Quiesced snapshots of the virtual machine
- Performance data in XenCenter
- High performance drivers

> Whatever the case, if you are using XenServer as your hypervisor, you should install XenServer Tools on all the virtual machines in the XenDesktop architecture.
>
> XenServer Tools can be installed on Windows from
> `http://bit.ly/xstools`.

Hyper-V Tools

In terms of tools, Hyper-V uses a Windows server virtualization feature called Enlightened I/O. Enlightened I/O is the performance tweak analogous to hardware-assisted virtualization integration used in VMware and XenServer. Enlightened I/O is a virtualization technique that is aware of high-level protocols that can access the VMBus directly, bypassing any device emulation layer. This requires that the hypervisor and virtual machine be aware of each other so that the virtual machine can take advantage of accessing the VMbus directly.

Microsoft does provide similar performance-enhancing ability through what they call Enlightened I/O. The Enlightened I/O and the Hyper-V-aware kernel are turned on by installing the Hyper-V Integration Service. Hyper-V and the root / child partition architecture require a processor that includes HAV, which is provided with Intel VT and AMD-V technologies. Hyper-V takes advantage of the processor hardware-assisted virtualization available from Intel and AMD. Microsoft and Hyper-V do not use paravirtualization techniques.

The enlightenments made with both the server (Windows Server 2008, 2012) and client operating systems (Windows Vista, 7, 8, 10) provide drivers and components that improve performance when accessing disk, memory, and video resources. For the Hyper-V Enlightened I/O to work, it must be enabled in the Windows server, and the Windows client must be "Enlightened" as well.

Turning on Hyper-V Enlightened I/O provides the virtual machine with the following:

- Improved disk performance
- Support for up to four processors on a virtual machine
- Hardware-assisted virtualization support in the processor

The Azure Cloud runs on a customized implementation of Hyper-V. If you are using Hyper-V as your hypervisor, you should enable the Enlightened I/O Integration Services in the server and make sure the client operating system supports Enlightened I/O.

For more information on Hyper-V, visit http://bit.ly/hypervIO.

Summary

Installing the hypervisor virtualization tools onto a virtual machine is always a good idea, regardless of the hypervisor vendor or VM operating system. You need the tools to give your VMs enhanced network drivers, a disk driver, memory management, and integration with the hypervisor for powering machines on and off. In the next chapter, we discuss networking.

4
Memory Optimization

In the first, second, and third chapters we defined some basic XenDesktop architectures, terminology, concepts, and components, and we covered how to size them. Then, we learned the basic building block of virtualization–the hypervisor. Now that we have a blueprint, we can take a look at all the pinch points or places where we might want to focus on optimization, starting with virtual memory. In this chapter, we will cover the following:

- XenDesktop nugget
- Hypervisor memory optimization
- VMware virtual memory
- XenServer virtual memory
- Hyper-V virtual memory

XenDesktop® nugget

Don't skimp on memory. Make sure each of your virtual machines have been allocated more than adequate amounts of memory with headroom so that you can avoid the hypervisor memory management techniques. As more and more VDI deployments pop up, you will see that large static memory allocations are necessary to get the best performance.

Hypervisor memory optimization

Hypervisors have certainly come a long way over the years. As of late, hypervisor vendors have gained enough traction in the market that they have wielded relationships with CPU and chip manufacturers such as Intel, AMD, and NVidia, in addition to the memory, storage, and network manufacturers. Today, when you go to buy a machine to run a hypervisor, there are built-in integrations between the hypervisor software and the physical hardware.

As of this writing, there are two types of hypervisors: Type-1 and Type-2. Also, there are four publicly available and usable hypervisors: VMware vSphere/ESXi, Citrix XenServer, Microsoft Hyper-V, and Linux open source **Kernel Virtual Machine (KVM)**. XenDesktop is only supported on ESXi, XenServer, and Hyper-V, so we will limit our discussion to those.

No two physical server architectures are the same, and there is more than one server vendor. Some of these vendors you are familiar with, such as **Hewlett Packard (HP)**, Dell, IBM, SuperMicro, and so on. While the server vendors all have different hardware architectures, they have four components in common that all operate with the same–memory, CPU, disk, and networking. The reason most of these server components operate in the same way is because they are all provided by other vendors in the marketplace who abide by relative adherence to industry standards. As such, we will break down each core component and discuss how the hypervisor can be optimized for that particular component.

Memory

As you can guess, with virtualization and the concept of collapsing multiple virtual machines into one physical server, there will be resource contention. The first issue that comes to mind is how all these virtual machines will share the memory resources in the server. If they can't, then there really is no point to virtualization.

The concept of sharing memory is critical to virtualization. Sharing memory happens natively in virtualization through different techniques that the 3qdh hypervisor implements, and we will discuss those. Sharing memory resources is different than overcommitting, in that it refers to the sharing of available memory.

The concept of overcommitting physical memory allows allocation of memory to virtual machines that exceeds the capacity of the physical memory in the system. Memory overcommitment assumes that some of the virtual machines will not be maximizing their use of allocated memory. This means that excess physical memory will be available for the hypervisor to dish out to other virtual machines. There is always a risk that you will be running too many virtual machines with too much memory overcommitment, so make sure you adequately allocate memory plus headroom to the virtual machines.

 Tribal Knowledge says that overcommitting memory, along with other resources, can be considered normal for server virtualization. However, in VDI, this could kill performance because usage patterns differ. It is always best to allocate enough memory with headroom so that you don't have to rely on overcommitting.

VMware

As you can guess, having a bunch of virtual machines requiring their own dedicated memory can add up. The benefit of virtualization is the concept of memory overcommitment, which allows a hypervisor to allow more memory to be shared with other virtual machines. Allowing basic memory sharing with or without memory overcommitment requires some mechanism to manage which virtual machine gets which block of memory and when. VMware uses memory reclamation techniques to manage this process. These techniques include transparent page sharing, ballooning, and host swapping.

Memory overhead

Memory overhead is the additional amount of memory required to allocate and access memory for a virtual machine combined with the extra memory space needed for the hypervisor to perform its magic.

Memory overhead in VMware is, on average, between 1 percent and 19 percent of allocated memory for virtual machines using one vCPU to eight vCPUs, respectively. We factor in quite a lot more for breathing room in the sizing spreadsheet, and you can adjust this value if required.

Transparent page sharing

Transparent page sharing (**TPS**) relies on the fact that, with many virtual machines running at the same time, some of them will have identical memory content. This gives way to sharing memory across multiple virtual machines in addition to within a single virtual machine. Hashing is a common technique in the industry to quickly and efficiently store and compare large chunks of data, in memory or on disk. Hashing takes a huge chunk of data and computes a hash value that is significantly smaller in size, yet repeatable every time. You will find hash table management deep within just about every piece of software these days. The VMware ESXi hypervisor uses hashing to identify matches of paged memory between virtual machines. If there is a match, it then performs a complete page memory comparison to be absolutely sure, and swaps the page out.

The upside to TPS is that the hypervisor can reclaim redundant copies of memory pages and keep one shared copy. Total memory consumption is reduced, leaving a larger amount of memory available to then be used for overcommitment. There is an additional **copy-on-write** (**CoW**) and page fault mechanism to ensure that virtual machines can modify shared pages of memory without disrupting other virtual machines sharing the same memory.

The following diagram explains the process:

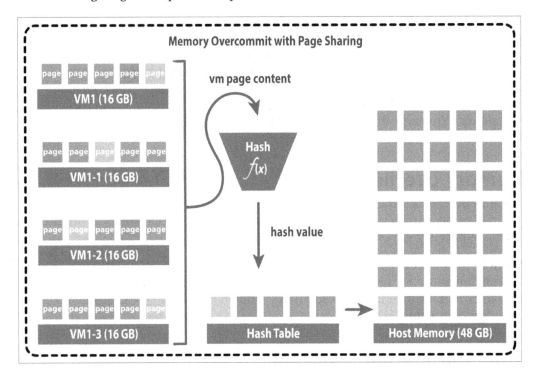

[TPS is no longer enabled by default in VMware due to a perceived security risk.]

There are some settings that can be used to tune TPS, which can be found in the **Advanced settings** under the **Mem** section. Default values are generated automatically and adjusted dynamically during runtime, so you can set it and forget it if you want.

Keep in mind that there is some overhead with TPS and it is dependent upon the scan rate and sharable memory across all VMs:

Parameter	Description	Default
Mem. ShareScanTime	This is the time taken to scan the virtual machine's entire guest memory.	60 min
Mem. ShareScanGHz	This is the scan rate in MB/sec per GHz of host CPU	4 GHz
Mem. ShareRateMax	This is the per-VM upper limit on the page share scan rate in pages/sec	1024 pages/sec

Mem.ShareScanTime and Mem.ShareRateMax can be disabled by setting them to a value of 0.

Ballooning

Ballooning is also a memory reclamation method; however, it is a little different. This is useful when the total amount of free host memory becomes low. A balloon driver is loaded seamlessly into the guest operating system, yet the guest VM doesn't have access to the driver. The driver exists for the sole purpose of communicating how much memory the guest can use for its balloon. The balloon driver asks the hypervisor how much memory it can use for ballooning, and the hypervisor returns a target size of the balloon that the guest can use. The balloon allows the guest operating system to inflate its memory usage to the target size. This becomes useful when the hypervisor host system starts to get low on memory. When this happens, the hypervisor artificially inflates the VM's balloon so that it consumes less memory on the hypervisor host but uses more memory inside its VM. The effect is the transfer of memory pressure to the VM. This gives the VM more headroom and also places the decision to swap out pages of memory onto the VM, relieving the hypervisor of having to do that task for every VM. Keep in mind that the overhead with ballooning is that it depends on the response time of the VM to actively allocate memory. So, if both your VM and the hypervisor are performing slowly, this may not help.

The following screenshot shows the ballooning process in hypervisor inflates balloon, vm allocates memory, and hypervisor releases host memory:

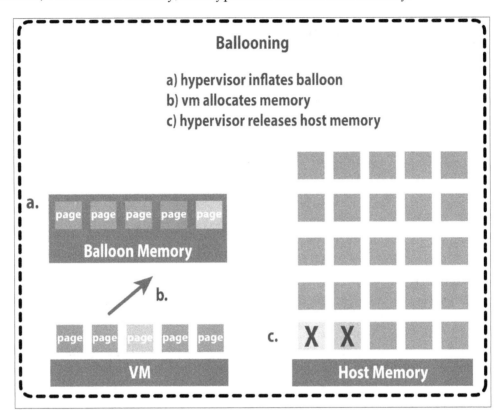

Tribal Knowledge says that ballooning can help in normal server virtualization. For VDI, you need to allocate more than enough memory so you don't get to ballooning conditions as this will negatively affect performance.

Hypervisor swapping

If transparent page sharing and ballooning aren't enough, VMware can use hypervisor swapping. Hypervisor swapping is a method where the hypervisor creates a separate swap file for each VM. If need be, the hypervisor can completely swap out the VM's physical memory to the swap file, freeing up memory to be used for other VMs. Hypervisor swapping is a brute force method but it is an efficient way to reclaim memory in a short amount of time for the hypervisor's sake. However, it can have a detrimental effect on VM performance.

The downside is that the hypervisor could start to randomly swap out VM memory pages without knowing which pages are critical to the VM's functioning, so it could potentially swap out critical pages and cripple a VM.

 Tribal Knowledge says that VM swapping will negatively affect the performance of VDI no matter what the storage medium. Allowing hypervisor swapping would be very bad.

There is yet another downside to this. If both the hypervisor host and the VM are memory constrained, there is a good chance that the hypervisor will swap out the VM's memory to the host swap space, while the VM has also swapped out the same page of memory to its own swap space. This phenomenon is known as double paging. Because of this, hypervisor swapping is a last resort mechanism for memory reclamation. The following diagram explains the swapping process:

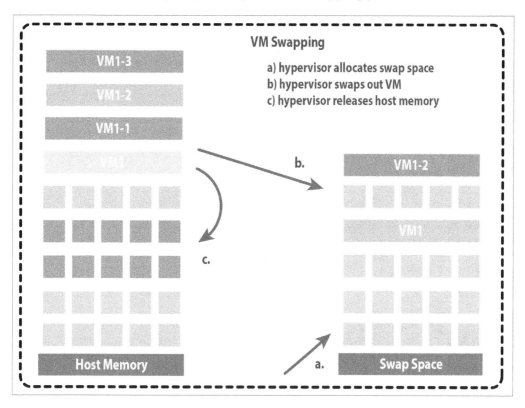

Compression

If all these techniques don't work, memory compression sets in. Memory is compressed by a factor of 2:1 and placed in a compression cache in the VM's memory. When the page is accessed, it is decompressed. Memory is fast and cheap, so compression/decompression in memory doesn't incur much overhead.

How memory reclamation works

There are a few mechanisms for memory reclamation at work under the covers. The first condition is when the total VM memory usage is less than the amount of memory allocated. Transparent page sharing happens automatically as the hypervisor can free up memory with little overhead.

Ballooning depends on the state of free memory in the hypervisor host. There are four hypervisor host memory states: high, soft, hard, and low. These have default thresholds of 6%, 4%, 2%, and 1% and are described in the following table:

Memory state	Description	Threshold setting
High	This is the total amount of hypervisor host free memory	6%
Soft	This is the total amount of hypervisor host free memory	4%
Hard	This is the total amount of hypervisor host free memory	2%
Low	This is the total amount of hypervisor host free memory	1%

In the high state, the hypervisor will not reclaim memory using ballooning or hypervisor swapping. If the total hypervisor host memory drops to the soft threshold, the hypervisor starts to reclaim memory using ballooning.

 Ballooning actually starts to happen before the soft threshold is reached because it takes time for the balloon driver to allocate and pin VM memory.

If ballooning doesn't work or the hypervisor free memory drops toward the hard threshold, the hypervisor starts to use hypervisor swapping in addition to ballooning. This is a brute force event that reclaims memory fast in an effort to get the host back to the soft state.

If memory drops below the low threshold, the hypervisor starts to reclaim memory using hypervisor swapping and blocks all virtual machines from taking more memory than they have been allocated. This doesn't happen very often.

The second condition is when the total VM memory usage is greater than the amount of memory allocated. In this case, the hypervisor will use hypervisor swapping and ballooning to reclaim memory from the VMs until their memory usage falls back to its allocated target. So, it is important to allocate adequate memory to your VMs because when this kicks in, it will choke the performance.

Virtual machine memory allocation

There are three parameters that you can configure to control virtual machine memory allocation, listed in the following table:

Parameter	Description	Default
Shares	This is a proportion of host physical memory	Normal
Reservation	The is the lower bound amount of physical memory allowed	0 MB
Limit	The is the upper bound amount of physical host memory allowed	Unlimited MB
Working size	This is the amount of virtual machine physical memory actively being used	Computed

ESX computes a memory allocation target for each VM based on its share entitlement, its estimated working memory size, limit, and reservation. The VM's memory allocation target is its consumed host physical memory size with added headroom given by the following formula:

Max memory allocation target = min [VMs memory size, VMs limit]

When host memory is overcommitted, a virtual machine's allocation target is between its specified reservation and its specified limit depending on shares and system load. Memory overcommitment happens when the virtual machine's memory usage is greater than its max memory allocation target. During an overcommitment condition, the hypervisor uses ballooning or hypervisor swapping to reclaim memory–a brute force effort. The decision between ballooning and swapping comes back to the states of high, soft, hard, and low. Also, during overcommitment, the hypervisor reclaims memory starting with the virtual machine that has the lowest number of shares per allocated memory page. If some virtual machines are idle, they are hit with an idle-tax to keep the shares-to-memory page ratio in check and prevent the hypervisor from swapping out memory from virtual machines that have a high share allocation but are not doing anything. If the memory isn't being used, there is no reason to keep it allocated to an idle virtual machine.

Here, we will discuss some caveats when working with VMware. In normal server virtualization, you would not want to disable page sharing or the balloon driver. They used to be enabled by default and provide greater efficiency with the lowest amount of overhead and impact to the entire system. However, in VDI, it is recommended to allocate enough memory to a virtual machine so that you don't have to use page sharing or ballooning.

Be careful with the limit and reservation parameters. Set the limit too low, and a virtual machine will start ballooning and swapping. Set the reservation too high, and a virtual machine will consume memory it doesn't need that could be used for other virtual machines.

The hypervisor host memory should be larger than the virtual memory usage. This is sort of a no-brainer, but it makes sense because if the virtual machine consumes more than the hypervisor host is capable of, ESX will start hypervisor swapping and ballooning unnecessarily, which could cripple your server.

Use shares to tweak performance. If virtual machine memory is too low and you have performance issues, you can play with the shares parameter to give the virtual machine a higher priority on hypervisor memory allocation.

Lastly, make sure the virtual machine memory size is just larger than the average virtual machine memory usage. The extra headroom will buffer against spikes, peaks, and bruises.

XenServer®

Similar to VMware, XenServer has some memory management techniques it uses to share physical memory resources. XenServer uses a technique called **Dynamic Memory Control (DMC)**.

Memory overhead

Memory overhead in XenServer is, on average, 1% to 4% of the virtual machine's static memory maximum value. We factor in quite a lot more for in the sizing spreadsheet for breathing room, and you can adjust this value if required.

Memory overhead calculation

Fortunately, in XenServer, there are some command-line utilities that allow you to view the overhead properties of your VM, so this gives you a useful tool to factor in realistic overhead values into your sizing.

One command that is useful is the host and VM memory computation command, illustrated in the following table:

Command line	Description
`xe host-compute-memory-overhead host=<host>`	This calculates the memory overhead of a virtual machine defined by its `host` ID
`xe vm-compute-memory-overhead vm=<vm>`	This calculates the memory overhead of a virtual machine defined by its `vm` ID

More API calls and command-line utilities for XenServer can be found at `http://wiki.xenserver.org`.

Dynamic Memory Control

As you can see from the previous discussion, VMware has a plethora of techniques built into their ESXi hypervisor for managing memory. Xen or XenServer takes a different approach. Xen or XenServer uses a technique called DMC to manage memory usage and overcommitment. There are two values of interest: the minimum and the maximum. The chunk of memory in between is called the **Dynamic Memory Range (DMR)**.

As you can guess, the minimum value is the lowest amount of memory available to the VM, and the maximum value is the highest amount of memory available to the VM. VMs run with their maximum memory value. When there is memory pressure on the hypervisor host, the Xen hypervisor will proportionally inflate the balloon driver on the VMs that have DMC configured until it has reclaimed enough memory to run efficiently.

The concept of ballooning is the same for XenServer as it is for ESXi. However, DMC actually gives you control over how that balloon operates with regard to the VM's allocated memory.

DMC can be modified on each VM during runtime, which is a huge benefit, because without it, you would have to change memory parameters and reboot the server.

So, when you are taking into consideration the amount of memory on each hypervisor host, you need to factor in the DMR. Start with the maximum value as a first VM; this gives you more flexibility should you need to run more VMs later on. The following table illustrates the concept using some simple math by dividing the total physical memory available on the server by the minimum and maximum values for DMR:

DMR min–max (GB)	Server physical memory (RAM GB)	VMs per server
1 ~ 2	128	128 ~ 64
2 ~ 4	128	64 ~ 32
4 ~ 6	128	32 ~ 21
4 ~ 8	128	32 ~ 16

Dynamic memory mode

Whenever you configure a DMC you are telling the hypervisor to pick a target memory allocation for the virtual machine and to meet that target. DMC is a feature that enables dynamic reallocation of memory between VMs using what is called the DMR.

Target memory mode

You can configure a specific memory target for the virtual machine, and the hypervisor will try to meet that target allocation for the VM. This could be useful in environments where you know precisely how much memory a virtual machine will use.

The difference between DMR and target memory is that DMR provides more flexibility to the host hypervisor in terms of managing physical memory. You could essentially set the DMR to be the same as the target memory by setting the dynamic minimum equal to the dynamic maximum.

Static Memory Maximum

All virtual machines in XenServer can be set with a **Static Memory Maximum** (**SMM**). Setting a SMM tells the hypervisor to never exceed that amount of memory allocation to a virtual machine under any circumstance. This can only be changed when the virtual machine is shut down. One thing to consider if you plan on having all virtual machines up and running on the host at the same time is that the XenServer hypervisor will never allow the sum of the Dynamic Memory Minimums of the virtual machines to exceed the physical memory plus overhead.

Hyper-V

Hyper-V uses a memory allocation technique that allows virtual machines to consume memory dynamically based on the current workload. This allows you to overcommit memory to run more virtual machines than you have memory for.

Memory overhead

Memory overhead in Microsoft Hyper-V is, on average, between 1% to 10% of the hypervisor host's total system memory. The hypervisor host needs around 2 GB to do its magic. The first VM needs 32 MB of extra memory, and every gigabyte of extra memory after that needs an additional 8 MB of memory. We factor in quite a lot more in the sizing spreadsheet for breathing room, and you can adjust this value if required.

Static memory

Static memory for Hyper-V has a different meaning than the true meaning of static memory microchips. Static memory is just that–a fixed amount of memory assigned to a virtual machine. In some cases, static memory allocation may not provide the best performance, but there are some workloads that only work with static memory such as Exchange, SQL, and Sharepoint.

Dynamic memory

Dynamic memory is Hyper-V's memory management technique for virtualization. Hyper-V does not use memory overcommitment. Hyper-V also uses the concept of Smart Paging that uses disk resources as additional, temporary memory when more memory is required. So, it makes more sense to say that Hyper-V uses dynamic memory to manage memory demand, without the expense of competing memory management techniques.

With dynamic memory, drivers are installed with the VM that communicate with the hypervisor to tell the VM how much memory it can use. In dynamic memory, you can set values for Startup RAM, Maximum RAM, Memory Buffer %, and Memory Weight.

Startup RAM or Minimum RAM defines how much memory the VM will be allocated when it is powered on. Maximum RAM defines how much memory the VM will be allowed to balloon up to. Memory Buffer % is an amount over and above the amount of memory the VM is using. So, if a VM is using 2 GB of memory and the Memory Buffer is at 25%, it will effectively use 3,072 GB.

> Some virtual machines, such as Active Directory Domain Controllers, need a lot of RAM at startup, and then usage declines over time.

The Memory Buffer is not guaranteed; however, it is an indicator of how much memory you want the virtual machine to request from the hypervisor when the VM needs more memory. In Hyper-V, virtual machines start out with the Startup RAM allocation and grab more dynamically using the Memory Buffer % as they encounter memory pressure.

Memory Weight is a priority value. This value determines which virtual machines actually get more memory when hypervisor memory pressure is high. Higher priority virtual machines get allocated extra memory first before lower priority virtual machines.

One thing to take note of is that the total virtual machine Startup RAM running cannot exceed the host physical RAM in Hyper-V. In other words, you can't overcommit Startup RAM past the physical RAM barrier.

One of the obvious familiar tools for monitoring virtual machine memory usage is the **Performance** tab in Task Manager.

Be sure to check the sizing spreadsheet for the `vRAMHeadroom` variable when doing your calculations for all the hypervisors.

> Also, make sure you download the sizing spreadsheet for all the detailed calculations you will need for appropriate sizing.

Again, the spreadsheet with calculations for building your architecture is available at `http://bit.ly/xdp-sizing`.

Summary

You should now have a good grasp of how memory is utilized by each of the three hypervisors used with XenDesktop–VMware ESXi, Citrix XenServer, and Microsoft Hyper-V. This chapter serves as a good reference to look back on as you build and size your system. Each hypervisor has different overhead and minimum memory requirements even when memory overcommitment is in use. In the next chapter, we'll discuss network optimization.

5
Network Optimization

You've learned about XenDesktop architectures, terminology, concepts, components, and sizing, as well as the fundamental component–the hypervisor. You've also learned about memory optimization and how the hypervisor can be the bottleneck or the key to performance. Now, we will look at how the virtual hardware operates in relation to XenDesktop with regard to networking. In this chapter, we will cover:

- The XenDesktop nugget
- Network virtualization
- Traffic separation
- Quality of service
- VMware virtual networking
- XenServer virtual networking
- Hyper-V virtual networking

XenDesktop® nugget

Network traffic in XenDesktop is not that high. In a steady state test, traffic on a single NIC for 5,000 users peaked at 2 Gbps for the desktop VMs, under 2 Gbps for XenDesktop virtual servers, less than 200 Mbps for hypervisor traffic, and slightly more than 10 Mbps for XenDesktop delivery controller traffic.

 The test referenced in the preceding paragraph can be found at
`http://bit.ly/xdp5k`.

If you outfit your servers with 10 **Gigabit Ethernet (GbE) Network Interface Cards (NICs)**, you should be safe and comfortable for existing and future network needs. For XenDesktop deployments of 1,000 users or less, you can probably get away with using just 1 GbE NIC in your servers.

Network virtualization

As we saw from earlier chapters, hardware virtualization is a challenge. Virtualizing the network is also a challenge. If you think about it, when we collapse computers into virtual machines, the networks they had been connected to are no longer physical switches and routers. In the virtualization world, the networks are collapsed and virtualized as well.

Network virtualization is the process of combining hardware and software network resources, such as routers and switches, into software-based entities that are run inside the physical machine. In other words, think about connecting a server's NIC to a physical switch using an Ethernet cable and assigning the computer to a VLAN. Now, think of that computer running as a virtual machine and creating a logical connection from a virtual network interface card to an internal software based switch, and then assigning the VLAN there. The concept seems fairly simple to imagine; however, the details surrounding the new paradigm for the network are fairly complex.

The virtual network now resides inside the physical server, and provides the communication path for virtual machines to connect and communicate using virtual Ethernet ports. When those virtual machines need to communicate with resources outside of the virtual infrastructure, they need to use the physical network resources such as the NIC. This is where it gets tricky because as we talked about in the memory optimization chapter, any physical network interfaces need to be shared among all the virtual machines. While it may prove to be a challenge, providing the ability to assign multiple Ethernet adapters across multiple virtual machines is also powerful.

Traffic separation

Some concepts play well with optimization no matter what hypervisor you are running. Traffic separation is one of those concepts. It is a good idea to separate your traffic into separate network interfaces for performance and manageability reasons. Two port 10 GbE interface cards are becoming more of a commodity, so you best look into using those. 10 GbE and 1 GbE NICs are common now, and it used to be that when we only had 100 MbE interface cards, Citrix recommended separating traffic in the following way:

Interface	Traffic type
Network Interface 1	Management/HA
Network Interface 2	Virtual machine traffic
Network Interface 3	iSCSI/NFS/NAS/Backup
Network Interface 4	Provisioning

Now, with the proliferation of higher speed networks that are 10 GbE and 1 GbE, separating traffic is a thing of the past and not really recommended.

If your traffic requirements are low enough that you won't saturate a 10 GbE interface, you could conceptually have one 10 GbE NIC and use VLANs to separate traffic. The Virtual Switches inside the hypervisors support VLANs.

 10 GbE NICs are becoming more of a commodity. 100 GbE interfaces are showing up on datacenter switches. Do yourself a favor and invest in 10 GbE NICs for your hypervisor hosts.

QoS

The most appropriate place to discuss **quality of service (QoS)** is in the networking section. We discuss QoS for XenDesktop here.

ICA/HDX virtual channels

Citrix supports QoS with the ICA/HDX protocol, and it is supported in the Citrix Receiver, as well. Within the ICA/HDX protocol, they have what are called virtual channels. Virtual channels exist so that control can be applied to specific functions such as printing, audio, keyboard, mouse, video, drive mapping, and so on. There are 32 maximum channels available for each ICA/HDX session. The following diagram shows the architecture of virtual channel:

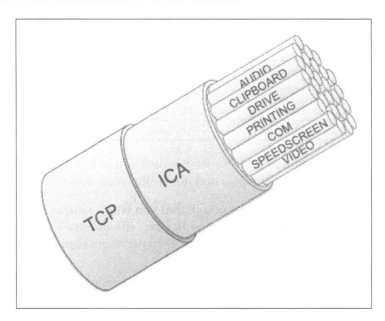

Multi-stream and multi-port

Multi-stream ICA/HDX provides the ability to configure multiple TCP connections to carry the ICA/HDX traffic between client and server. You can have up to four independent TCP streams, and up to five independent UDP streams. Each of these streams can be associated with a different class of service for QoS.

You can configure the class of service for each stream by assigning each stream to a unique port number and then assigning a priority to the stream. There are four possible priorities that can be assigned to each stream. There are four TCP streams available and five UDP streams available; however, the settings that are available to each stream are called either Primary or Secondary. There can only be one Primary stream.

You can then configure an additional class of service for each virtual channel within the stream. The separation of ICA/HDX traffic into multiple streams allows you to apply QoS prioritizations to the individual components of the ICA/HDX stream– hence, multi-stream QoS.

The following are the configurable priorities for each ICA/HDX virtual channel within a TCP stream:

- 0 = Very high priority
- 1 = High priority
- 2 = Medium priority
- 3 = Low priority

The following table illustrates the default values for each ICA/HDX virtual channel:

Channel name	Description	Multi-stream priority
CTXCAM	Client audio mapping	0
CTXTWI	Seamless Windows screen update data (ThinWire)	1
CTXCTL	Citrix control virtual channel	1
CTXEUEM	End user experience monitoring	1
CTXFLASH	Citrix flash redirection	2
CTXGUSB	USB redirection	2
CTXSCRD	Smartcard	1
CTXCLIP	Clipboard	2
CTXLIC	License management	1
CTXPN	Program neighborhood	1
CTXTW	Remote Windows screen update (ThinWire)	1
CTXVFM	Video server	1
CTXCCM	Client COM port mapping	3
CTXCDM	Client drive mapping	2
CTXMM	Citrix Windows multimedia redirection	2
CTXCM	Client management (auto update)	3
CTXCOM1	Printer mapping (thin client)	3
CTXCOM2	Printer mapping (thin client)	3
CTXCPM	Printer mapping (spooling clients)	3

Channel name	Description	Multi-stream priority
CTXLPT1	Printer mapping (non-spooling thin client)	3
CTXLPT2	Printer mapping (non-spooling thin client)	3
OEMOEM	Used by OEMs	3
OEMOEM2	Used by OEMs	3

Multi-stream policy settings

Multi-stream and multi-port settings must be enabled in the Group Policy Editor. It must be enabled for both the multi-stream computer configuration on the server side connections and for the multi-stream user configuration on the client side.

 Citrix warns that enabling multi-stream in conjunction with bandwidth limit policy settings, such as the overall session bandwidth limit, may produce unexpected results.

Multi-stream registry settings

The multi-stream settings can be tweaked using the **Registry** settings on the XenDesktop server and client.

The multi-stream registry key can be found at the HKLM\SYSTEM\ CurrentControlSet\Control\Terminal Server\Wds\icawd\MultiStreamIca registry.

Streams

The Streams sub-key refers to the ICA/HDX TCP streams. The format is Stream#, Stream Type, where Stream# can be the values 0, 1, 2, and 3, and Stream Type can be either P for Primary or S for Secondary. There can be only one Primary stream.

Virtual Channels

The Virtual Channels sub-key refers to the virtual channel stream pairs. The format is VirtualChannelName, Stream#, where VirtualChannelName is the ICA/HDX virtual channel identifier, and Stream# is the stream number that it should use.

The default installation would look like the following:

```
CTXCAM ,0; CTXTW ,1; CTXTWI,1; CTXLIC,1; CTXVFM,1; CTXPN ,1;
CTXSBR,1; CTXSCRD,1; CTXCTL ,1; CTXEUEM,1; CTXMM 2; CTXFLSH,2;
CTXGUSB,2; CTXCLIP,2; CTXCDM ,2; CTXCCM ,3; CTXCM,3; CTXLPT1,3;
CTXLPT2,3; CTXCOM1,3; CTXCOM2,3; CTXCPM ,3; OEMOEM ,3; OEMOEM2,3
```

Virtual networking

In virtual networking, virtual machines have virtual Ethernet adapters that connect to Virtual Switches. Everything found in a physical Ethernet adapter can be found in a virtual Ethernet adapter, and everything found in a physical Ethernet switch can be found in a virtual Ethernet switch.

Virtual Ethernet adapters

Essentially, a virtual Ethernet adapter is an emulation of the physical Ethernet adapter. Emulation is slow, so it is better to use an optimized paravirtualized Ethernet adapter. To take advantage of the performance gains in the paravirtualized adapter, you need to install the tools that are provided by the hypervisor manufacturer. Virtual network adapters have their own MAC addresses and unicast/multicast/broadcast filters and are strictly Layer 2 devices.

 Both the **Speed** and **Duplex** settings on virtual Ethernet adapters are irrelevant because the entire data transfer takes place in the host system's RAM instantaneously, without the pesky collisions and signaling issues found in physical mediums.

Virtual Switches

A Virtual Switch, or vSwitch, is similar to a physical switch but is software-based. It maintains a MAC-to-port forwarding table just like a physical switch. It uses the **virtual Forwarding Information Base (vFIB)** to look up the Ethernet frame's destination MAC address when it arrives and forwards the Ethernet frame to one or more ports.

All the benefits of the physical switch apply to the vSwitch. For example, vSwitches support assigning a virtual port to a single VLAN, also known as an access port in the physical switch realm. They also support assigning a port to multiple VLANs, alternatively known as a trunk port in the physical switch realm.

There are some real benefits to vSwitches. For example, because the vSwitch is in memory and there is only one, there is no possibility of connecting two vSwitches together, either accidentally or intentionally. Therefore, there is no need for the **Spanning Tree Protocol (STP)** as there is no possibility of a network loop.

One benefit of the vSwitch is that since all the virtual machines are in a single host, the hypervisor already knows all the virtual MAC addresses. This reduces the amount of time required to build a vFIB.

Uplink ports are virtual ports associated with physical network adapters that provide a connection between a virtual network and a physical network. Not all virtual ports need to connect to an Uplink. You could have internal switch VLANs just for virtual machine communication. Internal vSwitch ports do not need to connect to an Uplink or physical adapter to communicate with other vSwitch ports. Physical network adapters provide the communication connection between the virtual and physical world. Physical network adapters can be used with VLANs for single VLAN or VLAN Trunking. Similar to the physical networking world, if you want two virtual network ports to communicate using VLANs, they must be on the same VLAN. If they are on different VLANs and you want them to communicate, then you must configure a Layer 3 router to route the packets between the VLANs. The Vyatta open source router is a perfect way to do this as it runs inside a virtual machine.

VMware virtual networking

VMware includes a virtual networking infrastructure. The virtual networking, consisting of virtual machine ports and Virtual Switches, runs in ESXi–the hypervisor. VMware virtual ports and switches support VLANs that adhere to industry standards. A virtual machine can be configured with one or more virtual Ethernet adapters, each having its own MAC and IP address. Essentially, virtual machines have the same properties as physical machines from a networking viewpoint.

VM DirectPath I/O

VM DirectPath I/O is a VMware technology that can be used by virtual machines to directly access the underlying hardware, bypassing the hypervisor. This is a big performance improvement for virtual machines that are doing a lot of I/O processing. Some virtual machine functions get disabled when using this setting, such as memory overcommitment and page sharing, so be careful when configuring it.

VMware vSphere **DirectPath I/O (DPIO)** is a vSphere feature that takes advantage of VT enabled processors installed in ESXi hosts in order to improve performance for virtual machines. A processor feature in some Intel and AMD CPUs referred to as **I/O Memory Management Unit (IOMMU)** remaps **direct memory access (DMA)** transfers and device interrupts. This allows virtual machines to bypass the VMkernel and gain direct access to physical hardware.

VMDirectPath I/O is supported on most physical Ethernet adapters, but not all vendors support it, so be sure to check.

Tribal Knowledge says that you can experiment with DirectPath I/O, but only if you need additional performance throughput. In some cases, this might negatively affect performance as it disables some of the native functions of the VMware hypervisor.

VMDirectPath can be configured in the VMware vSphere Client under **Configuration | Advanced Settings**. The device must be rebooted before it takes effect (showing a green icon). Configurations are stored in the `/etc/vmware/esx.conf` file.

Make sure you have enabled the VT-d virtualization options in the server BIOS or you won't be able to perform VMDirectPath I/O. To do this without rebooting the server, type in the command `# esxcfg-info | grep HV Support` in the hypervisor host command line.

Network I/O Control

VMware Network I/O Control (NetIOC) provides a software-based approach to partitioning physical network bandwidth among the different types of traffic flows. It uses QoS policies to predict and prioritize network flows. There are different types of traffic that you may want to partition such as Management Traffic, Virtual Machine Traffic, vMotion Traffic, FT Traffic iSCSI Traffic, and NFS Traffic. NetIOC allows you to run multiple types of traffic on a single network pipe by allowing you to partition the traffic based on its priority. The NetIOC is only supported in the VMware **vNetwork Distributed Switch (vDS** or **dvSwitch)**, as opposed to the VMware **vNetwork Standard Switch (vSS** or **vSwitch)**.

vSwitch is a short name for Virtual Switch, which represents networking entities that connect virtual machines at virtual Layer 2 inside the ESXi hypervisor. The vSwitch is connected to the NIC(s) on the ESXi host.

dvSwitch is an enhanced vswitch, similar in functionality to the vSwitch; however, it is configured and managed centrally on the vCenter Server.

The vSwitch is a legacy technology in that it needs to be configured on the ESXi host. If you have multiple ESXi hosts, you need to maintain consistent configurations across those hosts manually. The dvSwitch is more up-to-date in that the switch configurations are done in vCenter Server–providing the same functionality as vSwitches with newer features.

NetIOC can be configured in the vSphere client in the **Resource Allocation** tab of the vDS by navigating to **Home | Inventory | Networking | Properties | Enable NetIOC** on this vDS. This is also where you can configure the limits and shares for each traffic type. **Limits** place a limit on the bandwidth of a specific traffic flow, and **Shares** allow traffic flows to share bandwidth of other underutilized flows.

Load Based Teaming (**LBT**) is an optimization policy enforcement scheme that makes sure the vDS Uplink capacity is optimized. It does this by moving a traffic flow to another port group that is less busy when it detects an Uplink that exceeds 75 percent of capacity over a 30 second period.

VMXNET 3

Virtual machines can be configured to use different types of virtual NICs that have different drivers built for them. Not all virtual NIC drivers perform the same. VMware will recommend that you use the VMXNET 3 virtual NIC because it contains the latest and greatest generation of paravirtualized code for high performance. VMXNET 3 includes features such as receiving side scaling for TCP/IP, IPv4 and IPv6 offloads, and MSI/MSI-X interrupt delivery. It supports adaptive interrupt coalescing to drive high throughput to VMs; however, in high latency environments, it is recommended that you disable interrupt coalescing.

The available network interface types are explained in the following table:

Virtual NIC type	Description
E1000	Emulated version of the Intel 82545EM GbE NIC, with drivers already available in guest OSs.
Flexible	Boots as a Vlance adapter, but with VMware Tools, installed upgrades itself to the VMXNET adapter.

Virtual NIC type	Description
Vlance	Emulated version of AMD 79C970 PCnet32 Lance, Inc. This is an older 10 Mbps NIC using 32 bit operating systems at most.
VMXNET	Optimized for performance in a virtual machine. You must install VMware Tools to use this driver.
VMXNET2	An Enhanced VMXNET driver that supports jumbo frames and hardware offload.
VMXNET	The next generation of paravirtualized NICs designed for high performance. Supports all of VNXNET2 plus support for Receive Side Scaling in Windows, IPv6, and MSI/MSI-X interrupt delivery.

Large Receive Offload

Large Receive Offload (LRO) uses larger buffers and fewer packets and can improve performance. What it does is reassembles packets into larger buffers and sends a lower number of packets to the virtual machines, but the packets are larger. This frees up the vCPU to be used on other processes. The downside is that if the virtual machine can't handle the extra large packets, it could cause performance degradation.

Port Groups

Port Groups are groups of ports on a Virtual Switch. A Port Group is a management object for aggregation of multiple ports on a Virtual Switch that serves as a connection point for virtual machines. There are several configuration options under a Port Group. All VMs connected to the same Port Group can communicate with each other, but it does not have the benefits of a VLAN that separates the broadcast domain. Virtual machines in different Port Groups on different networks can communicate with each other because of this, and this isn't ideal. Ideally, you need to create VLANs to provide network isolation between Port Groups. You can assign VLAN IDs to Port Groups.

Virtual Switch VLAN

Virtual Switch VLAN Tagging (VST) occurs when you assign a VLAN ID to a Port Group and the virtual machine's packets get tagged with the VLAN ID when they leave the VM, and packets that arrive at the VM are untagged.

Virtual Guest VLAN Tagging

Virtual Guest VLAN Tagging (VGT) allows virtual machines connected to a Port Group to tag and untag packets with VLANs from within the virtual machine operating system. To make this work, you assign VLAN ID 4095 to the Port Group, which tells the Port Group to view all VLAN IDs. This can be thought of as VLAN Trunking for a vSwitch.

External Switch Tagging

External Switch Tagging is transparent to the ESXi hypervisor, and is where packets get VLAN tagged when they leave the ESXi host and reach the physical switch, and are untagged when they leave the physical switch and arrive at the ESXi host.

If you are planning on using VST or VGT on a a vSwitch that is connected to a physical external switch through an Uplink physical adapter on the ESXi host, you will need to configure the physical switch port that the Uplink is connected to in trunk mode.

NIC Teaming

NIC Teaming allows you to connect a single vSwitch to multiple physical Ethernet adapters. A NIC team can share the load of traffic between physical and virtual networks among some or all of the members. This also provides for passive failover in the event of a physical switch hardware failure or network outage. You apply NIC Teaming policies at the Port Group level.

[All physical switch ports on a NIC Team must be in the same Layer 2 broadcast domain.]

Load balancing

Load balancing allows you to spread network traffic from virtual machines on a vSwitch across two or more physical Ethernet adapters in the hypervisor host. This gives you a performance boost because you have the benefit of throughput from more than one Ethernet adapter.

There are several load balancing algorithms available to you, as follows:

- **Route based on the originating vSwitch port ID**: It allows you to tell the packets to go back out on the virtual port they entered. This is also known as persistent load balancing, which makes sure that packets enter and leave on the same virtual and physical Ethernet ports. This provides an extra level of performance and has the lowest compute load on the ESXi server.

- **Route based on source MAC Hash**: If you choose this algorithm, the packets will be sent to the same physical Ethernet adapter based on a hash of the source Ethernet MAC address. This provides a level of persistency but takes up valuable processor time as the hash needs to be computed.

- **Route based on IP Hash**: This algorithm hashes both the source and destination IP address of the packets and sends packets to the same physical Ethernet adapter, but again will cost you in terms of computing the hash value.

Link aggregation

Link aggregation is based on an industry standard IEEE 802.3ad specification, which allows you to group together multiple physical Ethernet adapters. Link aggregation uses the **Link Aggregation Control Protocol (LACP)**. Link aggregation can provide an extra level of performance if your physical Ethernet adapter is reaching its capacity.

Failover protection

NIC Teaming provides a level of failover protection if one or more physical Ethernet adapters fail. If you do this, you will need to tweak the following options on the physical Ethernet switch to avoid possible delays:

Parameter	Description	Setting
Spanning Tree Protocol (STP)	Nicknamed Spamming Tree Protocol, this will take a switch port out of service if you're not careful, and it takes a lot of processing power.	Disable
Etherchannel	PAgP or LACP must be disabled because they are not supported.	Disable
Trunking	VLAN Trunking uses precious processing power. (Saves 4 seconds).	Disable

If you're using Cisco switches, enable PortFast mode for access interfaces and PortFast trunk mode for trunk interfaces (this saves 30 seconds).

VMware networking maximums

Just because virtual networks are no longer bound by physical limitations doesn't mean they are limitless. Most software packages have limitations built-in to keep resources manageable. Virtual networking software has limits, and the limits for VMware virtual networking are listed in the following table:

Device	Max
Virtual Ethernet adapters per virtual machine	4
vSwitch ports per hypervisor host	4,096
vSwitch ports per vSwitch	1,016
vSwitches per hypervisor host	248
Uplinks per vSwitch	32
Port Groups per vSwitch	512
1 GbE physical Ethernet adapters per hypervisor host	8~32 depending on vendor
10 GbE physical Ethernet adapters per hypervisor host	8
40 GbE physical Ethernet adapters per hypervisor host	4
VMDirectPath PCI/PCIe devices per host	8
SR-IOV number of virtual functions	4,096
SR-IOV number of 10 GbE NICs	8
VMDirectPath PCI/PCIe devices per virtual machine	64

VMware networking tweaks

Networking in VMware works great by default in 90% of the cases. For higher performance, it will take some tweaking and effort.

There isn't a "one size fits all" deployment, but here are some tweaks for VMware networking that apply to XenDesktop:

Method	Setting
VMDirectPath	Use VMDirectPath I/O to bypass the hypervisor.
vSwitch uplink teaming	Use uplink teaming, but make sure you use an efficient load balancing algorithm that doesn't compute expensive hashing.
NetIOC	Use NetIOC to make sure traffic flows don't oversaturate links.
Separate IP networks	Place different traffic flows on different physical (NIC) and logical (IP) networks.
Interrupt coalescing	Disable interrupt coalescing with the following command: `# esxcli system module parameters set -m ixgbe -p InterruptThrottleRate=0.`
VMXNET 3	Use the VMXNET 3 virtual NIC as it has the best paravirtualized NIC drivers for high performance
Disable Virtual Interrupt VMXNET 3	Disable interrupt coalescing on the virtual NIC in vSphere: **Client** | **VM Settings** | **Options** | **Advanced General** | **Configuration Parameters**. Enter the parameter `ethernetX.coalescing = disabled`.
Disable Virtual Interrupt for all virtual NICs	In vSphere Client, go to **Configuration** | **Advanced Settings** | **Net**. Set `CoalesceDefaultOn = 0`.
Disable interrupt moderation for physical NICs	Use the command line, enter `# esxcli system module parameters set –m <driver> -p "param=val"` to disable interrupt coalescing on the physical network adapters.
Large Receive Offload	Disable LRO using the following command line: `# modprobe -r vmxnet3; modprobe vmxnet3 disable_lro=1`
10 GbE & 40 GbE physical Ethernet adapters	10 GbE and higher physical Ethernet adapters are becoming a commodity. Buy larger pipes and your networking life will be easier.

XenServer® networking

XenServer networking isn't that much different from VMware as it also features methods to connect virtual machines to external networks, internal networks, and VLAN networks. Virtual machines have virtual network interface cards or adapters connected to networks using virtual NICs. Virtual NICs connect to vSwitches inside XenServer that connect to other virtual networks and external physical networks.

Virtual networking in XenServer is not that much different than networking in the physical realm. You assign virtual interfaces to a virtual machine and configure them with both an IP address and a MAC address–although, a MAC is assigned by default. The internal vSwitch networks your virtual machines and allows them to connect to external physical switches through the physical Ethernet adapter.

The sequence of configuring networking on XenServer is important and should match on all XenServer hosts to maintain ease of manageability. Networking is also a XenServer Pool function. You create a pool that has all the virtual machines defined and you then create networks inside those pools.

Ever since XenServer 6.0 was released, it used Open vSwitch as the open source vSwitch. Before this, it used Linux bridge networking.

Open vSwitch was developed by Nicira, which was purchased by VMware and is now part of their NSX platform. Open vSwitch continues to be supported. Open vSwitch is now a production quality, multilayer switch licensed under the Apache 2.0 License. It supports standard protocols and management interfaces and distribution across multiple physical servers similar to VMware's **vNetwork Distributed Switch (vDS)**.

XenServer® networking maximums

XenServer has its limitations, as well, and the limits for XenServer virtual networking are in the following table:

Virtual machine device	Max
Virtual NICs per virtual machine	343

XenServer host device	Max
Physical NICs per host	16
Physical NICs per network bond	4
Virtual NICs per host	512
VLANs per host	800

XenServer resource pool device	Max
VLANs per resource pool	800
Active hosts per cross-server private network	16
Cross-server private networks per resource pool	16
Cross-server private network virtual NICs per resource pool	256
Hosts per vSwitch controller	1,024
Virtual machines per vSwitch controller	1,024

XenServer® networking tweaks

Networking in XenServer is similar to VMware in that it is not optimized by default. It requires some tweaking and effort to make it perform. There isn't a "one size fits all" deployment, but here are some tweaks for XenServer networking that apply to XenDesktop:

Method	Setting
irqbalance	Enabled by default, this distributes processing of dom0-level interrupts across all available Dom0 vCPUs, and not just the first one. It is also beneficial to use at least 4 vCPUs for the XenServer hypervisor.
Dom0 vCPUs	Increases the number of Dom0 vCPUs.

Queue length	Increases the send queue length to 1,024 using the following command:
	
	`vif-list`
	
	`ifconfig vif<X>.<Y> txqueuelen 1024.`

SR-IOV and IOMMU	Enables SR-IOV and IOMMU.
CPU affinity	Sets CPU affinity to vCPU 1 because all interrupts will be processed on vCPU 0.
GRO and LRO	Disables **Generic Receive Offload** (**GRO**) and **Large Receive Offload** (**LRO**). Experience shows it lowers the overall Dom0 throughput.

Method	Setting
Receive side copying–desktops	Enables RSC for desktop virtual machines. The offload benefit to the VM desktop is valuable to the Dom0 vCPU. Create a new registry key in the virtual machine using the following command: `\HKEY_LOCAL_MACHINE\SYSTEM\CurrentControlSet\services\xenvif\Parameters, DWORD named ReceiveMaximumProtocol = 1.`
Receive side copying–other VMs	Disables RSC for all other VMs. Lets the Dom0 vCPU handle the traffic throughput. Create a new registry key in the virtual machine using the following command: `\HKEY_LOCAL_MACHINE\SYSTEM\CurrentControlSet\services\xenvif\Parameters, DWORD named ReceiveMaximumProtocol = 0.`
Jumbo frames	
NIC offloading	Enables NIC offloading.
Netback threads	Changes netback threads in Dom0.
10 GbE & 40 GbE physical Ethernet adapters	10 GbE and higher physical Ethernet adapters are becoming a commodity. Buy larger pipes and your networking life will be easier.

Hyper-V networking

Hyper-V Network Virtualization provides virtual networks to virtual machines. The Hyper-V vSwitch is a software-based Layer 2 network switch that is available in the Hyper-V Virtual Network Manager, which is available in the Hyper-V Manager when you install the Hyper-V Server Role. Hyper-V virtual networking is a robust solution with four major components. Windows Azure Pack for Windows server provides a tenant-facing portal to create virtual networks. The System Center 2012 R2 Virtual Machine Manager provides centralized management of the virtual networks. Hyper-V Network Virtualization provides the infrastructure needed to virtualize network traffic. Hyper-V Network Virtualization gateways provide connections between virtual and physical networks.

Hyper-V includes some robust features for multi-tenant deployment of virtual machines, such as isolated private VLANs to establish isolated tenant communities. Most of the advanced multi-tenant features are not necessary for XenDesktop, unless you are going to be providing XenDesktop as a service to multiple organizations in the same server infrastructure.

 Windows Azure is Microsoft's Cloud, similar to Amazon Web Services or Rackspace. Azure is based on Hyper-V. An upside to using Hyper-V locally and Azure in the cloud is that you can migrate virtual machines from your local datacenter to the Azure cloud seamlessly.

There are three types of networks in a Hyper-V virtual network. An external virtual network allows you to bind to an external physical network adapter so that virtual machines can communicate with systems on the physical network. The external virtual network needs to be bound to a physical network adapter that is connected to an external Layer 2 physical switch. The internal virtual network allows communication between virtual machines on the same virtual network and on the same virtualization host. A private virtual network is the same as an internal virtual network, but does not allow communication between the Hyper-V host and the individual virtual machines on the private network.

There are two network adapters or NICs available to virtual machines in Hyper-V. The default network adapter provides the best performance and gets enabled when you install integration services. The legacy network adapter is only needed for PXE boot and operating systems that don't support the VMBus NIC, and has some performance limitations because it is an emulated driver.

 VMBus is a logical inter-partition communication channel that allows virtual machines to access hardware resources faster, but it can only be available when you install Microsoft Integration Services into the virtual machines running on Hyper-V.

One thing to keep in mind when using Hyper-V is that the moment you create a network device, it automatically creates a new vSwitch.

Hyper-V networking maximums

Hyper-V vSwitch has its limitations, as well, and the limits for the Hyper-V vSwitch are in the following table:

Virtual machine device	Max
Virtual NICs per virtual machine running the default network adapter.	8 VMBUS NICs

Hyper-V server	Max
Physical NICs per host	Unlimited
NIC Teaming (bonding)	Unlimited
vSwitches per server	Unlimited
Virtual network switch ports	Unlimited
VLANs	4,095
Virtual machines per VLAN	Unlimited

 While Microsoft claims there is no limit to the above resources for marketing purposes, the reality is that there is going to eventually be a limit based on available computing resources.

Hyper-V networking tweaks

There are some capabilities of the Hyper-V vSwitch that can actually benefit a XenDesktop deployment, such as the following:

- Bandwidth limit and burst support has two settings. Bandwidth minimum guarantees an amount of bandwidth reserved. Bandwidth maximum caps the amount of bandwidth a VM can consume. These options are set per VM.

- **Explicit Congestion Notification (ECN)** marking, also known as **Datacenter TCP (DCTCP)**, enables the physical switch and the operating system to regulate traffic flow such that the buffer resources of the switch are not flooded, resulting in increased traffic throughput.

One setting that might be useful is the **Bandwidth Management** setting for the virtual network adapter. If you open the virtual network adapter in Hyper-V, you will see a section called **Bandwidth Management**. Here, you can set minimum and maximum bandwidth in megabytes per second. This can help keep noisy virtual machines from starving the bandwidth on the Hyper-V host, but you should not need to do this for XenDesktop.

- **Virtual Machine Queue** (**VMQ**) is an Intel technology that allows a NIC to transfer incoming packets directly to the NIC's receive buffer using direct memory access. VMQ should be enabled by default. When VMQ is enabled, a dedicated queue is established on the physical network adapter for each virtual network adapter that has requested a queue. As packets arrive for a virtual network adapter, the physical network adapter places them in that network adapter's queue.

  VMQ provides improved networking performance for the management operating system as a whole rather than to a specific virtual machine. For best results, treat queues as a scarce, carefully managed resource. Because queues are allocated to virtual machines on a first-come, first-served basis, making all virtual machines eligible for a queue may result in some queues being given to virtual machines with light traffic instead of those with heavier traffic. Enable VMQ only for those virtual machines with the heaviest inbound traffic. Because VMQ primarily improves receive-side performance, providing queues for virtual machines that receive the most packets provides the most benefit to overall management operating system performance.

- **TCP Offload Engine** (**TOE**) is designed to improve network performance by implementing the entire TCP/IP stack in hardware rather than in software. Offload also reduces traffic on the PCI bus of the server. If you are using NIC Teaming, you will want to disable offload features. Tribal Knowledge from the field says that TCP offload features are only useful on physical NICs, not virtual NICs. You will want to enable this on the Hyper-V server NICs and disable TCP offloading on virtual NICs.

The `Large Send Offload` parameter is enabled/disabled in the network adapter properties on the **Advanced** tab. The `Disable Task Offload` parameter is disabled by adding a `DWORD` set to a value of 1 in the `HKEY_LOCAL_MACHINE\SYSTEM\CurrentControlSet\ Services\Tcpip\Parameters` registry section of the virtual machine.

Hyper-V 2012 running on a Windows Server 2012 includes a new feature called Logical Networks, which is enabled in System Center Virtual Machine Manager SP1. Logical Networks allow you to create multiple virtual networks on a Hyper-V host to isolate network traffic without the configuration hassle of VLANs. Logical Networks support the use of fibre channel network adapters on the Hyper-V host. SR-IOV is supported on Windows Server 2012, as well.

Use jumbo frames. Jumbo Ethernet frames send 9,014 bytes in each packet, compared to 1,500 in a standard frame Ethernet. Make sure every component in the network uses jumbo frames.

In Hyper-V 2008 R2, you are limited to one virtual NIC in the parent hypervisor partition. In Hyper-V 2012 R2, you can create multiple virtual NICs in the parent partition.

Hyper-V 2012/2012 R2 supports Single Root I/O Virtualization (SR-IOV) capable network adapters.

Summary

Networking in the virtual world is a bit different than we are used to, but it's not that hard to get your arms around it. Networking with any of the hypervisors can be done, and with good performance, if you understand each of their unique ways of doing it. This chapter taught you how to understand their networking idiosyncrasies and gave you some performance tips. Similarly, hypervisors handle virtual storage differently. In the next chapter, we discuss virtual storage optimization.

6
Storage Optimization

Arguably, the most important and most talked about topic surrounding virtualization is storage. There are many different types of storage, so we will review them and find out which one is the best for XenDesktop and virtualization. Then there is the controversial subject of **Input/Output Operations Per Second (IOPS)**. You must have heard about it by now, and IOPS certainly deserves a discussion. There are some interesting solutions to this problem and we will discuss them here as well. In this chapter, we will cover:

- XenDesktop nugget
- IOPS
- Storage types
- Storage virtualization
- VMware storage
- XenServer storage
- Hyper-V storage

XenDesktop® nugget

Arguably, the biggest bottleneck in XenDesktop is storage, specifically IOPS. You can buy fast storage, but will still need to battle the IOPS problem. There are some interesting solutions to the IOPS problem being provided by other companies and startups and we will discuss these later in the chapter. Until these are baked into hypervisors and drivers as a standard feature, you will likely need to look at some of the specialized vendors offering a solution to this problem.

Historically, to get good storage performance, you would install the hypervisor onto the local drive and put all of your virtualized resources, such as XenDesktop and its army of virtual machines, onto network shared storage such as iSCSI SAN or **Fibre Channel over Ethernet (FCoE)**. However, recent Tribal Knowledge says that you get better performance by using fast locally attached storage with solutions such as Fusion IO or HP Accelerator cards that provide SSD class performance.

While PvDisk saves on storage space, it is really only necessary to use this if you want to provide personalized desktops with user-specific, user-installable applications. If you have a good workspace manager, like AppSense, you can personalize non-persistent desktops and, in most cases, combine them with persistent VDI for a smaller group of users.

Input/output operations per second

Input/Output operations per second is a commonly talked about measurement of performance with regards to storage. It was mentioned early in this chapter; so think about how you will be impacted by IOPS. For Lab and Proof of Concept deployments, IOPS may not affect you that much. If you are deploying XenDesktop for production use, IOPS adds up and it will affect you.

If you think about it, this makes sense. Before virtualization, you had one person or just a handful, accessing the hard drive for data. Now, you have hundreds or thousands of users accessing hard drive data and storage was never really engineered for that type of usage. The industry and some startups are just now getting around to solving the problem.

For regular virtualization environments this problem is almost non-existent – but for SBC and VDI it does exist. It would also be nice to virtualize the I/O traffic flow for regular office workers (with local resources) versus VDI users (where the desktop lives in the datacenter) and SBC users (where multiple users share a virtual XenApp server).

You can tune and tweak your storage performance, but you may want to look into some third party solutions that solve the IOPS problem specifically. I know there is one company that solves the problem using proprietary de-duplication and compression algorithms and another company solves the IOPS problem by analyzing the blend of the read and write operations. These companies will be discussed later in the chapter.

When it comes to IOPS, SATA drives are slow and provide less IOPS, while SCSI or SAS drives are faster and provide higher IOPS. Also, depending on the SSD manufacturer, SSD's can be the fastest of them all. Whichever storage methodology you choose, be sure to check to make sure that it supports a large number of IOPS. Also, ask to see the independent third party test report, because performance numbers published by a vendor are always better in the marketing glossy than they are in the real world.

We also need to mention something about IOPS patterns. It is worth looking into IOPS patterns for different types of workloads. For example, IOPS patterns for databases are different from IOPS patterns for VDI workloads. IOPS for the VDI desktop is dependent on the type and number of applications being used, and the services inside the desktop VM. IOPS for VDI is also dependent on how much users interact with their virtual desktop. Light users, such as ones using only email, Microsoft Office, and web browsing typically consume 5 IOPS. Heavy users, with large PowerPoint, Word, and Excel files that perform heavy operations, can have 15 IOPS. IOPS are factored into the sizing spreadsheet we provide at the beginning of the book.

Also worth mentioning is the read/write ratio. The read/write ratio is the ratio of the number of read operations versus the number of write operations. For VDI, the read/write ratio can be anywhere from 50/50 to 20/80 depending on the workload.

 Tribal Knowledge says that if you don't know your read/write ratio, assume normal 50/50 to heavy 20/80 ratios when designing.

In addition, keep in mind the RAID Penalty. There are different RAID levels, as you know, and each one will add an additional amount of time depending on the RAID level, because, for example, if you have multiple disks configured in RAID, the write operation has to happen on multiple disks. This effect is called a RAID Penalty. The RAID Penalty can be factored into the IOPS calculation using the following formula:

*IOPS = VM Read IOPS + (VM Write IOPS * RAID Penalty)*

The following table lists each RAID Penalty:

RAID level	Penalty
RAID 0	0
RAID 1	2
RAID 5	4
RAID 6	6
RAID 10	2
RAID DP	2

Data de-duplication

There are some startup companies that offer data de-duplication technologies to increase IOPS. Microsoft has implemented its own feature for this. Per volume data de-duplication is built into Windows Server 2012 and is available for any data stored on NTFS volumes.

 Data de-duplication is not available for boot drives or live SQL databases. Live VMs are supported for de-duplication in VDI.

Personal vDisk

Machine Creation Services (**MCS**) is a XenDesktop deployment technology that allows you to create a single, golden image to be used as a virtual desktop by all of the users. **Personal Virtual Disk** (**PvD**) is a feature of XenDesktop that allows you to expand on that by providing an extra user-specific data-disk where the user can store their unique data including profiles and applications. What this means is, MCS with PvD allows you to use a single operating system image for a number of virtual machines, instead of creating a separate disk for each virtual machine while providing a mechanism for individual user preferences and customizations to the base image that will occur. PvD keeps track of these for each user on a P: drive and in the UserData.vhd file. The delta between the base image that is shared, and the user customizations that are stored, is large enough that it ends up saving you a lot of space and money on storage.

Storage types

As operating systems and methods to store data have evolved over the years, so have the different protocols, filesystems and methods for storing data. There is no one best method, but there are some to avoid when it comes to performance.

Block versus file

File storage has been around for a long time and is what is traditionally found in local hard disk storage systems. File storage is synonymous with **Network Attached Storage (NAS)** systems. In file storage the disk is configured with a protocol such as NFS or CIFS and files are read/written to disk using that protocol.

File storage types

File storage is synonymous with file level storage formats such as NFS (*nix) and CIFS (Windows) on locally attached media.

NFS (Network File System) is found on Unix and Linux systems. NFS was originally developed by SUN Microsystems and it allowed a client to access files on a server over a network. NFS is an open standard based on several RFCs. NFSv4 is the latest that you will find most commonly deployed, yet enhancements are being made to that as well. NFSv4 operates over TCP.

CIFS (Common Internet File System) is synonymous with Microsoft Windows. CIFS was developed by Microsoft and was also intended to allow clients to access files over a network. It was based on the **Server Message Block (SMB)** protocol, which is gaining support as a protocol of choice in Windows operating systems. XenDesktop only runs on Windows so you should be aware of this.

Block storage types

Block storage is synonymous with **Storage Area Network (SAN)** systems. Block storage uses volumes that can be created and accessed like individual disk systems as an abstraction to the underlying physical media. The volumes are referred to as Blocks. Volumes can be formatted for filesystem use with NFS, SMB, CIFS, and even **VMware File System (VMFS)**. In block storage, volumes are configured with a protocol such as **Internet Small Computer System Interface (iSCSI)** or **Fibre Channel over Ethernet (FCoE)** and blocks of data are read/written to the volume using that protocol. Volumes are formatted to use a file level format such as NFS or CIFS/SMB.

The **Small Computer System Interface** (**SCSI**) standard only allowed SCSI devices to talk to attached servers, a concept made popular by a company called Adaptec. SCSI required a proprietary interface card and interface cable. iSCSI is an Internet protocol-based storage networking standard built for linking together storage resources across a network. In other words, it is a way to allow SCSI devices to communicate over a network, specifically an IP network. iSCSI allowed clients to send SCSI commands over a network to storage devices on remote servers. It is considered a SAN technology. It gives servers the illusion that the iSCSI disks are in fact locally attached. iSCSI runs on the Internet protocol which makes it suitable for long distance network connections. iSCSI runs over existing IP networks.

Fibre Channel is a technology for transmitting data to storage devices at high data rates using optical fiber cable. It is three times as fast as SCSI and it uses optical fiber as a connection medium. Devices can be as far as six miles away from each other. FCoE encapsulates Fibre Channel frames over Ethernet allowing Fibre Channel access to high speed Ethernet networks. FCoE integrates directly with Ethernet by replacing its layer 0 and layer 1 frames with Ethernet frames. FCoE plugs in to the Ethernet protocol stack and has its own Ethertype, whereas iSCSI runs on top of IP in the stack. FCoE is therefore not routable and doesn't work across IP networks.

Local versus network

There was a time when you could store all of your data on local hard drives on the server. Times have changed and, with the explosion in the amount of data that applications use, it has become necessary to store data out on the network, where it is more flexible for adding capacity for large storage needs. You can use either or both for XenDesktop, but in large deployments, you may want to look at network storage.

Local storage

Local storage refers to disk drives attached directly to the computer by an embedded or attached interface. This is the traditional concept of a disk drive in a computer.

SATA or **Serial ATA** is locally attached storage and an evolution of the ATA interface which has **integrated drive electronics** (**IDE**) built into the disk drive itself. SATA was once a leading technology but is now considered slow. Despite the age, it is still widely used because it is cheap and throughput is good enough when compared to the throughput of a typical computer system bus available today.

SAS or **Serial Attached SCSI** is based on the SCSI standard which has been around for a few years. SCSI, pronounced scuzzy, is an advanced method for moving data between disks and computers, and is fast. You used to need a SCSI controller board plugged into an extra slot in the computer motherboard to use SCSI. SAS gets around that extra board and SCSI drives can now be embedded or part of the motherboard. SAS is fast, as SCSI as was, but it is expensive. Compared to the throughput rates of current motherboards, the cost may not outweigh the throughput benefit. NL-SAS is Near Line SAS which is basically a merging of SATA disks with a SAS controller.

SSD or **Solid State Disk** uses memory instead of magnetic spinning disks and is a recent innovation. It is mentioned here because you can now purchase SSD drives for your servers and you can order SSD storage arrays in appliances to be used as a SAN. There are no mechanical parts to an SSD which should reduce the failure rate. SSDs are fast yet expensive. SSDs are mentioned here because I am sure they will continue to drop in price and you will want to squeeze out any type of performance you can. If you can afford SSDs, use them, however be sure to compare prices as the cost per MB between SATA and SAS or SSD is quite different.

There are a couple of additional topics that need mentioning with regards to SSD. TRIM is a concept that was introduced shortly after SSDs were introduced. Trimming is a method to handle garbage collection on SSDs to reclaim sectors or pages that are no longer in use. Wear leveling is a technique for prolonging the service life of SSDs. EEPROM and Flash memory, which is what SSDs are based on, have a limited number of erase cycles before becoming unreliable. Wear leveling is a technique that works around that limitation to ensure erasures and re-writes are distributed evenly across the storage medium. This prevents any one single block from failing prematurely due to a high number of write operations.

In some cases SSD storage has been used for acceleration and caching as an addition to traditional SATA or SAS storage.

Network storage

Network storage refers to disk drives or storage that is part of an external appliance consisting of disk drives or storage arrays that are accessed over a network. Two types of systems come to mind and were discussed previously, SAN and NAS. NAS provides file-level storage and SAN provides block-level storage. NAS is considered good for personal use and would not scale for a XenDesktop deployment. SAN, on the other hand, is considered good for business use and would scale for a XenDesktop deployment.

One thing to keep in mind is that both SAN and NAS can scale significantly larger in terms of the number of drives and overall capacity that can be housed in a platform compared to local storage, however, some vendors offer expansion shelves for their servers, such as HP, proving that local storage is a fine option. SAN typically uses SCSI drives and NAS typically uses SATA drives.

If you are planning a small lab system, you will probably be able to get away with locally attached SATA disk drives in your server(s). If you are planning a large XenDesktop deployment you will probably need an external SCSI appliance that can be accessed with iSCSI, FCoE or Fibre Channel.

Hyper converged storage

Hyper converged storage is a software-defined approach to storage management that combines storage, computing, networking, and virtualization technologies into one physical unit that is managed as a single system. Hyper converged technologies are appealing and becoming more attractive as there is more control over the storage provisioning, providing a single pane of glass for management and allowing a horizontal scale-out model.

Redundant array of inexpensive disks

Redundant array of inexpensive disks (**RAID**) is a technology that has been around for a while and it aims to combine multiple disk drives into a single logical disk drive. RAID is really designed to provide redundancy and drive failure protection. The reality is that disk drives have mechanical parts and they fail. There are different levels of RAID providing differing levels of protection. The following table illustrates the different RAID technologies:

RAID Level	Protection scheme	Description
RAID 0	Striping, no mirroring or parity	No redundancy or disk failure protection. Striping distributes data equally among all disks in the set. Throughput of RAID 0 is fast because it equals the throughput of the disk multiplied by the number of disks in the array.
RAID 1	Data mirroring, no parity or striping	Data is written identically to all drives in the array producing a mirror set of drives. Throughput is slower than one of the drives because every drive must be updated.

RAID Level	Protection scheme	Description
RAID 2	Bit level striping and parity	Data is striped so that each sequential bit is on a different drive. Parity data is calculated on bits and stored on a separate parity drive.
RAID 3	Byte level striping and parity	Data is striped so that each sequential byte is on a different drive. Parity is calculated on bytes and stored on a separate drive.
RAID 4	Block level striping and parity	Replaced by NetApp with a proprietary format called RAID-DP.
RAID 5	Block level striping with distributed parity	Requires at least three disks. If you lose two drives, you lose all of your data. Parity data is distributed across all drives.
RAID 6	Block level striping with double distributed parity	Fault tolerance upto two failed drives. If you lose three drives, you lose your data. Parity data is distributed across all drives.
RAID 10	Disk mirroring and disk striping	Also known as RAID 1+0. Only 50% of total capacity of drives is usable. If you lose two disks in the same mirrored set, you lose all data. RAID 10 provides redundancy and performance.
RAID DP	Double disk failure protection.	Basically RAID 6 with data loss prevention using double parity based data protection.

Cloud storage technologies

When everything moved to the cloud, storage changed. The cloud providers realized they had to provide storage in enormous quantities with good performance. Old technology wouldn't do. Developers started to invent technology tailored to how software uses and stores its data – removing the dependency on the hardware. The thought was, just give me as much storage capacity as possible and I will take care of my redundancy and performance through software techniques. If a disk drive fails, just leave it, the data will be replicated elsewhere and recovered immediately on the fly – so there is no expensive rebuild time.

This topic is mentioned only because cloud storage providers use this type of technology. In fact, XenDesktop is supported in Amazon EC2 and on the Citrix CloudPlatform. One of the deployment models that will emerge is a hybrid model in which XenDesktop is deployed on a combination of private and cloud storage. One of the new technologies that Citrix recently announced is Citrix Workspace Cloud, which aims to deliver desktops and applications from the cloud.

Storage virtualization

There are a lot of moving parts in storage virtualization. Storage systems either provide block or file storage. Block storage typically uses iSCSI or FCoE while file storage typically uses NFS or CIFS/SMB. As virtualization abstracts the underlying hardware, so too does storage virtualization abstract the physical storage resources. Virtualization attempts to present the virtual machine with storage resources and then does the emulation or mapping to the actual physical storage location. The mapping of virtual to physical storage is maintained in a mapping table called meta-data.

The hypervisor uses the meta-data to map I/O requests from the logical location on the virtual disk into I/O requests on the physical disk. Storage virtualization allows logical storage representations to be aggregated into storage pools. This allows storage resources to scale up significantly and be transparent to the virtual machine using the storage. Logical disks or virtual disks are made visible to the virtual machine through the hypervisor. Storage virtualization combined with storage area networking creates a landscape for almost limitless storage resources.

Data migration is the ability to move an entire storage container such as a vdisk to another platform quickly. VMware has implemented such a technology called vMotion, while XenServer uses XenMotion. Data migration might not be that important to you in terms of a XenDesktop implementation, but may be of interest in your disaster recovery implementation.

Thin provisioning is a method of optimizing space on storage. Thin provisioning allocates space based on users' minimum requirements, and gives the appearance that there is actually more storage than is available or useable. This is a departure from traditional disk management techniques that used to require you to allocate the entire disk to the operating system requiring its use. Thin provisioning is a great fit for virtualization because it allows efficient use of resources for the most people.

Storage virtualization and pooling, along with thin provisioning, free up precious storage space that, on a traditional physical server, would be allocated entirely to the operating system, wasting free space.

Pooling is a storage virtualization technique that allows you to merge all physical storage resources into large logical storage volumes. The physical storage systems can be of different types. Pooling allows you to expand and contract storage by simply adding more storage or removing storage in the pool. When combined, storage pooling, thin provisioning, and data migration can bring new levels of productivity and flexibility to your virtual computing strategy.

A discussion of storage virtualization wouldn't be complete without mentioning some of the recent innovations being brought to market by individual companies. Interesting storage optimization solutions are being offered by Fusion IO (`www.fusionio.com`), Atlantis Computing (`www.atlantiscomputing.com`), Nutanix (`www.nutanix.com`), ThinIO (`http://thinscaletechnology.com/thinio/`), and SanDisk UltraDimm SSD Storage on RAM (`http://www.sandisk.com/enterprise/ulltradimm-ssd/`).

VMware virtual storage

VMware supports both file and block storage. Through vSphere, which includes the ESXi hypervisor, VMware provides features and APIs which offer an abstraction layer for physical storage resources to be addressed, managed, and optimized in a virtual environment.

Datastores

VMware vSphere allows you to create logical containers called datastores. Virtual machine operating systems and their data are stored in these containers. Datastores can also be used for storing `.iso` images, templates and other files.

Virtual machine filesystem

VMware has its own storage system format known as the **Virtual Machine File System** (**VMFS**). VMFS can be deployed on a SCSI-based local or networked storage device such as a SAN device. NFS is a filesystem from the *nix world and can be deployed on a NAS device.

VMFS allows multiple vSphere servers to access shared virtual machine storage concurrently and enables virtualization-based distributed architectures to operate across a cluster of vSphere servers. It is the basis for scaling beyond the limits of a single server's storage capacity. vSphere supports block-based storage on directly attached storage (SATA, SAS, SSD, Fibre Channel) and on networked SAN devices using FCoE and iSCSI. vSphere also supports file-based storage using the NFS storage format on local as well as networked NAS devices.

Some other benefits of a virtualized storage infrastructure include snapshots, which are a point in time copy of a virtual machine and its data for backup and recovery, live migration of running virtual machines from one physical server to another, automatic restart of a failed virtual machine on a different server, and clustering virtual machines across different physical servers.

Virtual machine storage

Virtual machines in VMware view their storage as common SCSI and/or IDE controllers so to the virtual machine looks and acts as if it is installed on its own dedicated server with directly attached local storage. The following diagram shows the architecture:

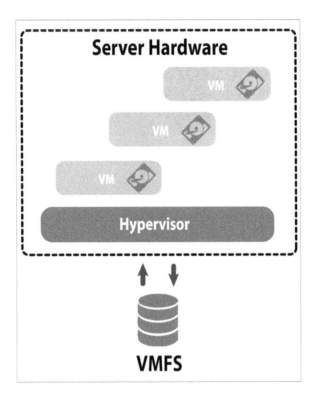

vMotion

VMware vMotion enables the live migration of running virtual machines from one physical server to another with zero downtime and transaction integrity. vMotion is transparent to end users.

VMware storage limits

When you create your virtual environment, you still need to be aware of the boundaries of the virtual and physical hardware. There are limitations to VMware storage and these are listed in the following table. These limits represent the maximum values attainable, have been tested by VMware, and are valid for vSphere 5.5.

Virtual machine limits

The following table shows the virtual machine limits:

Device	Max
Virtual SCSI adapters per virtual machine	4
Virtual SCSI targets per virtual SCSI adapter	225
Virtual SCSI targets per virtual machine	60
Virtual disks per virtual machine	60
Virtual disk size	62 TB
IDE controllers per virtual machine	1
IDE devices per virtual machine	256
Virtual SATA adapters per virtual machine	4
Virtual SATA devices per virtual SATA adapter	810,000

VMware ESXi host limits

The following table shows the VMware ESXi host limits:

Virtual Disks	Max
Virtual disks per host	2048
iSCSI	**Max**
LUNS per server	256
Qlogic iSCSI HBA initiator ports	4
Broadcom iSCSI HBA initiator ports	4
NICs bound to iSCSI stack	8
Total paths on server	1024
Total paths to a LUN	8
Qlogic dynamic targets per adapter	64
Qlogic static targets per adapter	64
Broadcom 1 Gb iSCSI targets per adapter	64
Broadcom 10 Gb iSCSI targets per adapter	128
Software iSCSI targets	256
NFS	**Max**
NFS mounts per host	256

Virtual Disks	Max
Fibre Channel	**Max**
LUNs per host	256
LUN size	64 TB
LUN IDs	255
Total paths to LUN	32
Total paths on server	1024
Total HBAs of any type	8
HBA ports	16
Targets per HBA	256
FCoE	**Max**
Software FCoE Adapters	4
VMFS	**Max**
Volume size	64 TB
Volumes per host	256
Hosts per volume	64
Powered on virtual machines per VMFS volume	2048
Concurrent vMotion ops per VMFS volume	128

More VMware configuration maximums can be found at `http://bit.ly/vmwmaxs`.

VMware storage tweaks

VMware are continually improving their product, which means they are ahead of the game when it comes to tweaking storage performance. For example, you can have a virtual machine with a VMDK disk size of 62 TB. Some concepts related to storage performance in VMware are discussed in the following sections.

VSAN

We mentioned hyper converged storage earlier. VMware has a VSAN implementation that allows you to aggregate storage into a single resource pool that delivers high performance at a lower cost.

vFRC

VMware Flash Read Cache (**vFRC**) allows a hypervisor host to use a local **solid state drive** (**SSD**) as a cache for virtual machines. It can improve performance by caching in the SSD drives I/O loads that are heavy and need reduced latency. vFRC is enabled in the vSphere client.

CBRC

Content Based Read Caching (**CBRC**) is used in VDI deployments to reduce read I/Os sent to the storage system. This improves scalability of the storage system and is transparent to the virtual machine. CBRC is a 100% host-based and RAM-based caching solution and can really help with boot storms and A/V scans. CBRC can also really help reduce the IOPS load on the storage system.

Storage I/O Control

Storage I/O Control (**SIOC**) monitors end-to-end latency on a datastore, whereas SIOC throttles back the usage on virtual machines that are using excessive I/O. Different share values can be assigned to different VMs to prioritize access to the datastore. Just turning on SIOC ensures each VMDK has equal access to the datastore.

I/O Analyzer

VMware I/O Analyzer is a tool designed to measure storage performance in a virtual environment and to help diagnose storage performance concerns. I/O Analyzer is a virtual machine or virtual appliance that can be used to test storage and display results graphically. I/O Analyzer can use IOMeter to generate loads. I/O Analyzer can be found at `https://labs.vmware.com/flings/io-analyzer`.

SCSI Controller

When you create a virtual machine guest, the vSCSI Controllers that are presented are based on the drivers that are available in that OS distribution. For best performance, select the LSI Logic SAS or VMware **Paravirtual SCSI** (**PVSCSI**) controller. The PVSCSI or para-virtualized SCSI driver is the most efficient when it comes to virtual machines that have very I/O intensive operations. XenDesktop virtual machines can generate a lot of IOPS, so this is the best driver to use.

XenServer® virtual storage

XenServer supports both local storage in the form of SATA, SAS, and SSD. It also supports networked storage in the form of SAN and NAS. XenServer uses NFSv3 over TCP for remote file storage on NAS and iSCSI and Fibre Channel for block storage on SAN. Through XenCenter, which uses the XenAPI (xapi), XenServer provides an abstraction layer for physical storage resources to be addressed, managed, and optimized in a virtual environment.

[
 NFSv4 and NFX over UDP are not supported on XenServer
]

Repositories

Storage is organized as storage repositories in XenServer; these contain virtual disk images, physical block devices, and virtual block devices. In XenServer, a storage respository is an abstraction of the physical disk device, which can be either locally attached or on a SAN. Virtual disk images are created as a storage abstraction that can be presented to virtual machines for storage. The virtual machine sees this as a virtual disk. A XenServer **storage respository** (**SR**) is a storage container where virtual disks are stored and can be either a local disk, an NFS server or an iSCSI target. Common types of storage that are available for SRs in XenServer are NFS VHD storage and iSCSI storage over SAN.

A **Virtual Block Device** (**VBD**) is a representation of virtual storage respositories. SRs can be used to attach **Virtual Disk Images** (**VDI**) to virtual machines using a VBD. The virtual block devices appear to virtual machines as local block devices.

Blkfront, blkback, blktap, and tapdisk

You may recall from an earlier chapter that we discussed how XenServer para-virtualized virtual machines running in user space (DomU) to communicate with the kernel space (Dom0) using front end and back end drivers. The storage implementation is a good illustration of this concept. The virtual machine running in DomU uses blkfront to communicate with blkback in the hypervisor running in Dom0. Blkback in turn communicates with blktap running in Dom0 to page storage requests in memory before they are read/written to disk.

Blktap then hands this off to a tapdisk driver running in user space (DomU) which communicates with the disk storage system for reads and writes:

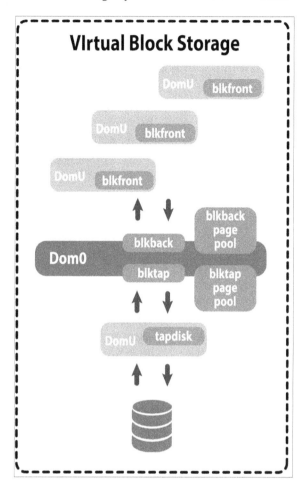

Tapdisk3

Tapdisk3 is a new storage implementation in XenServer, based on the open source Xen project. It has some significant improvements in performance. It connects directly to the Dom0 for disk and memory paging. The tapdisk3 data path improves performance 100% for writes and 150% for reads.

 The tapdisk3 storage driver is available in XenServer 6.5

Storage resource pools

A XenServer resource pool is a set of multiple XenServer installations that are bound together as a single entity managed in XenCenter. When a pool is deployed with a shared storage repository, virtual machines can be started on any XenServer host in the pool and can be dynamically moved between hosts during runtime using XenMotion. One of the hosts in the pool is designated as the pool master, and that controls all the activities in the pool. Resource pools can be a nice high availability feature if you build it in, because it automates many functions. For example, once a storage configuration is made in the pool, the pool master automatically propagates configuration changes to all member systems. This simplifies scaling up to quickly add more systems along with a high availability strategy.

> If you want high availability and XenMotion, use network shared storage such as an iSCSI or FCoE SAN

IntelliCache

IntelliCache caches data for a virtual machine shared master image in local storage on the hypervisor host. This is really helpful when multiple virtual machines share a common disk image, as in the case of a master image. There is a requirement that thin provisioning be enabled for IntelliCache to work.

> IntelliCache can be enabled during the XenServer installation by selecting **Enable thin provisioning optimized storage for XenDesktop**. You must enable this during installation as it cannot be done after installation. This feature is used with MSC and not PVS.

XenMotion®

XenMotion allows live migration of running virtual machines in a shared storage environment, such as a pool. For example, you can move a running virtual machine from one physical host to another without any disruption or downtime to the VM and its applications.

XenServer® storage limits

Even in XenServer, you still need to be aware of the boundaries of the virtual and physical hardware. There are limitations to XenServer storage and these are listed in the following tables.

Virtual machine limits

The following table shows the limits of virtual machines:

Device	Max
Virtual disk images (including CD-ROM)	4096
Virtual CD-ROM drives	1
Virtual Disk Size (NFS)	1996
Virtual Disk Size (LVM)	1996

XenServer® host limits

The following table shows the limits of a XenServer host:

Device	Max
Concurrent active virtual disks per host	2048

XenServer® pool limits

The following table shows the limits of XenServer Pool:

Device	Max
Paths to a LUN	8
Multipathed LUNs per host	25610
Multipathed LUNs per host for storage respositories	25610
Virtual Disk Images per storage repositories	600

XenMotion® limits

The following table shows the limits of XenMotion:

Device	Max
Virtual Disk Images per virtual machine	6
Snapshots per virtual machine	1
Concurrent transfers	3

XenServer® storage tweaks

XenServer storage performance can be monitored with a command line tool called xsiostat. Increasing the amount of data that can be in transit between the virtual machine and the storage repository at any given time will improve performance.

Sanbolic Melio

The SDx Platform from Sanbolic, whose Melio software has helped organizations worldwide realize the greatest value from their Citrix VDI deployments for many years, is a pure software-based SDS solution that allows customers to create their own (customized) storage systems using industry standard computing and storage components. Such systems, whose intelligence is delivered through the platform's advanced software stack, offer superior performance and scale-out capabilities (thousands of nodes and exabytes of storage capacity), as well as unparalleled resilience, at significantly lower cost than traditional hardware-based storage arrays.

Workload balancer

XenServer 6.5 includes a **Workload Balancing (WLB)** virtual appliance. It gives you deep insight into system performance and allows you to move workloads dynamically, based on CPU, storage and network load.

Storage buffer

As one of the bigger bottlenecks in the server architecture, storage needs a buffer between the storage medium and the memory. XenServer allows you to configure and increase the amount of storage buffer used on the host. If you increase the amount of storage buffer size to the limit of 256 block requests, it will improve storage performance throughput. This is especially important when running a large number of VM's.

Blkback page pool size

If the blkback page pool becomes full, throughput will be limited on the VBD. Increasing blkback will increase performance when large chunks of data are in transit and the blkback page pool becomes full. By default the blkback page pool is set to two full communication rings of 32 requests each.

This can be set to four or eight full rings per SR. The blkback page pool size can be set using the following commands:

```
# xesr-param-set uuid=<SR_UUID> \
other-configuration:blkback-mem-pool-size-rings=<NR>
```

NR is the number 2, 4, or 8.

Increasing the blkback page pool size to four doubles the amount of usable page pool grants per SR to 1408. Setting it to eight quadruples the amount of page pool grants to 2816 per SR. Using the default of two assigns 704 page pool grants per SR.

Blktap page pool size

If you increase blkback page pool size, you need to increase the blktap page pool size. This is done a little differently as there is no xe command to do it. To set the blktap page pool size, you need to edit the /opt/xensource/sm/blktap2.py file. By default, blktap page pool size is set to 704.

To set the blktap page pool size to 1408 pages per SR, try the following commands:

```
blktap.set_pool_name(sr_uuid)
blktap.set_pool_size(1408)
exceptOSError, e:
ife.errno == errno.EEXIST:
```

To set the blktap page pool size to 2816 pages per SR, try the following commands:

```
blktap.set_pool_name(sr_uuid)
blktap.set_pool_size(2816)
exceptOSError, e:
ife.errno == errno.EEXIST:
```

Communication rings

The blkback driver negotiates the number of communication rings with the blkfront driver. By default, the blkfront driver is set to 1 communication ring. It is possible to configure blkback to negotiate communication rings up to three for an eight page ring size, resulting in 11264 KB of data in transit at any time.

The following table illustrates the communication ring to data capacity relationship:

Rings	Ring size (pages)	Number of requests outstanding (pages)	Inflight data capacity
0 (default)	1	32	1408 KB
1	2	64	2816 KB
2	4	128	5632 KB
3	8	256	11264 KB

To enable multi-page rings in a hypervisor host, there are two places to edit:

- To enable inflight capacity to 11264 KB, change the `max_ring_page_order` parameter:

```
# cd /sys/module/blkbk/parameters
# echo 3 >max_ring_page_order
```

- To make the change persistent, edit the `/boot/extlinux.conf` file:

```
# cd /boot
# viextlinux.conf
label xe
# XenServer
kernel mboot.c32
append /boot/xen.gz mem=1024G
dom0_mem=752M,max:752M --- /boot/vmlinuz-2.6-xen
blkbk.max_ring_page_order=3 --- /boot/initrd-2.6
xen.img
```

 Tapdisk and blktap are not configurable at the time of this writing.

I/O scheduler

Different storage I/O schedulers will be applied based on the type of storage repository. You can change the I/O used on your SRs. You may have to contact the manufacturer of the storage to discover which one will work best. Cfg is commonly used for local disks and noop is used for iSCSI disks.

To find out which scheduler is being used for your SR, use the following commands:

```
Display the scheduler:
# cd /sys/block/sda/queue
# cat scheduler
The scheduler in brackets is currently in use:
noop anticipatory deadline [cfq]
```

To change the scheduler for your SR, use the following commands:

```
Display the scheduler:
# cd /sys/block/sda/queue
# echonoop> scheduler
# cat scheduler
Example output:
[noop] anticipatory deadline cfg
```

In addition, there are I/O scheduler options and configurable parameters available for each type of scheduler. For example, the parameters available for the CFQ scheduler can be found.

To display the I/O scheduler options use the following commands:

```
# cd /sys/block/sda/queue/iosched
# ls
```

Example output:

```
back_seek_maxfifo_expire_syncslice_asyncslice_syncback_seek_penaltylo
w_latencyslice_async_rqfifo_expire_async quantum slice_idle
```

> Use consistent high performance storage repositories across your deployment. Mixing local disks with iSCSI will cause XenServer to use the noop I/O Scheduler, which will starve the local disks of page requests and kill performance. If you end up mixing local and iSCSI storage, set the I/O scheduler to cfg to perform a fair allocation of page requests.

Hyper-V virtual storage

Microsoft's Hyper-V implements storage with flexible features. Hyper-V supports file storage in the form of a shared virtual hard disk, SMB 3.0. Hyper-V supports block storage with Fibre Channel and iSCSI storage arrays. Disks are presented to virtual machines as either a virtual IDE controller or a virtual SCSI controller.

Cluster Shared Volumes

Cluster Shared Volumes (CSV) is a feature of failover clustering introduced in Windows 2008 R2 for use with Hyper-V. A CSV is a shared disk containing an NTFS or ReFS (Windows Server 2012 R2) volume that is made accessible for read and write operations by all nodes within a Windows server failover cluster. This enables a virtual machine to have complete mobility throughout the cluster, as any node can access the VHD files on the shared volume. CSV simplifies storage by allowing large numbers of VMs to be accessed from a common shared disk and increases the resilience of the cluster by providing I/O fault detection and recovery over alternate communication paths between the nodes in the cluster.

Resilient filesystem

ReFS is proprietary to Microsoft and was introduced in Windows Server 2012 with the intention of replacing NTFS. The key design advantages include automatic integrity checking, data scrubbing, and protection against data degradation. It also includes built-in hard drive failure handling, redundancy, RAID, copy on write, long path, and filenames. Most importantly it includes features for storage virtualization and pooling which include an arbitrary logical volume size. ReFS aims to address major concerns with virtualization and storage going forward – volume size and reliability.

Live migration

While VMware has vMotion and XenServer has XenMotion, Hyper-V has live migration. Live migration allows you to move a running virtual machine from one SAN to another with no downtime. It also supports moving VMs from local to SAN and vice versa. There is another option called shared nothing live migration, where the VM and its data can be moved if it is not using shared storage. Moving the VMs data from one SAN to another is called storage live migration.

Storage spaces

Storage spaces is a storage abstraction layer that runs on top of the NTFS filesystem and uses SMB 3.0 to create a pool of storage from local or shared disk drives. Storage spaces can be thought of as a virtual SAN that pools different types of storage across various servers into a single unified storage resource.

Tiered spaces

Tiered spaces add to storage spaces by keeping the most frequently accessed data on **Solid State Storage (SSD)** or faster storage and keep less frequently accessed data on the slower drive mechanisms.

Disk storage types

The fixed size disk creates a **Virtual Hard Disk (VHD)** that is exactly the size you specify, allocating all of the data blocks plus the overhead required for VHD headers and footers.

The dynamically expanding disk is similar to thin provisioning. The initial allocation contains no data blocks. Space is dynamically written to the VHD up to the maximum size specified.

The differencing disk is a special type of dynamically expanding disk. It uses a parent/child topology where the parent disk remains unchanged and any write operations take place on the child disk. There is a lot of overhead in this type of disk, and it is not ideal for use in production.

The passthrough disk allows the virtual machine to bypass the Hyper-V hypervisor and access the disk directly. You must set the disk to offline in the Hyper-V settings. The performance gain with this type of disk is marginal and you can't use this with SQL.

Hyper-V storage limits

Hyper-V is based on the Windows server. Therefore, Hyper-V is constrained by the limits of the Windows operating system. Accordingly, the Windows server scales to many thousands of LUNs per host bus adapter.

Hyper-V storage tweaks

Hyper-V runs on top of the Windows server operating system and, as a default install, you can imagine that it might just not be optimized for virtualization. The following are some tweaks you can use to improve the storage performance in Hyper-V.

SMB Direct

SMB Direct is a new feature in Windows Server 2012 and 2012 R2 that supports adapters that have **Remote Direct Memory Access (RDMA)** capability. Network adapters with RDMA can function at full speed with very low latency using very little CPU. It allows remote storage to resemble local storage with the advantage of increased throughput, low latency, and low CPU utilization.

Storage drivers

Hyper-V runs on top of the Windows server. Therefore, if you've installed any iSCSI or Fibre Channel storage, make sure you have the latest high performance drivers installed before you install VMs

Unnecessary protocols

Disable unused protocols on the Hyper-V server network interface cards, such as IPv6, Discovery Mapper and Responder, and so on.

Default disk path

Under the Hyper-V settings window you can set the default disk path for virtual machines to map to your shared storage or iSCSI SAN. Just be sure to set it to something other than the c:\ drive to avoid filling up the system disk.

[If you are using CSV, the shared volume is actually a path on the c:\ drive.]

Storage controller

Use the virtual SCSI controller when selecting hard disk controllers for your virtual machines. For high I/O workloads, each VHD should be attached to a separate virtual SCSI controller for best performance.

Disk storage type

Of all the disk storage types available, Microsoft recommends a fixed size disk for the VHD, claiming that creating a disk that emulates a physical disk also creates all of the overhead for VHD headers and footers.

Storage QoS

To prevent virtual machines from hogging all of the IOPS, you can set the IOPS minimum and maximum values for your virtual machines. Storage QoS is configured at the VHDX layer. You can set this in the Hyper-V Manager, under the hard drive, advanced features.

Summary

Storage is likely one of the largest bottlenecks to contend with in virtualization. Always select the highest performance storage infrastructure. The safe bet is to install the hypervisor onto local storage and create all of your virtual machines on external networked storage such as iSCSI SAN, Fibre Channel, or Fibre Channel over Ethernet. In the next chapter, we will discuss CPU optimization.

7
CPU Optimization

A lot of information passes through the CPU, whether it's virtualized or not. When you install a hypervisor, it carves up the physical CPU into virtual CPUs. With the advent of hyper-threading, the number of vCPUs conceptually doubles. In addition, in virtualization, you can overcommit CPU resources to multiple virtual machines. In this chapter we will cover:

- XenDesktop nugget
- Intel and AMD virtualization technology
- CPU virtualization
- VMware virtual CPUs
- XenServer virtual CPUs
- Hyper-V virtual CPUs

XenDesktop® nugget

If you use the sizing spreadsheet calculator you shouldn't need to customize or change any CPU resource allocations on your virtual machines. You should be able to get good performance by allowing the hypervisor to manage CPU sharing and time-slicing.

Tribal Knowledge says you should allocate eight vCPUs to the host hypervisor for best performance, although you can probably get great performance with four. Refer to the article at http://bit.ly/xenscale.

Virtual CPUs

A **Virtual CPU (vCPU)** is an abstraction or representation of the physical CPU. As you can imagine, if you have hundreds, if not thousands, of virtual machines running on your servers, they will all be competing for the CPU. Luckily, the integration between the CPU manufacturers and the hypervisors means that these resources can be shared and overcommitted.

Virtual CPUs or vCPUs are assigned to virtual machines when you create them, either by the hypervisor virtual machine manager or by the CLI. The beautiful thing about vCPUs is that you can carve them up any way you see fit to meet your computing requirements.

In the early 1990's vCPUs had to be emulated, which is why many emulation techniques are still around as artifacts. All of the virtualization tasks were handled through software emulation, which was slow and inefficient. The next step was para-virtualization, which allowed virtual machines to bypass the hypervisor with APIs and still offer a performance advantage. Intel and AMD finally came to their senses and in 2005/2006, they modified their CPU architectures to adapt to virtualization technology. Both Intel and AMD created extensions to their processors to help virtualization achieve better performance and resource utilization.

Hyperthreading

The concept of hyperthreading also makes it appear that there are more virtual cores or vCPUs than there are physical cores. The way it works is that hyperthreading generates two logical CPUs that use the same scheduling mechanism. Keep in mind that the two logical CPUs are not as effective as a single physical core. Hyperthreading provides a mechanism to increase available resources. You can overcommit the number of cores you assign to a virtual machine in virtualization. Hyperthreading means you can overcommit even more.

 Tribal Knowledge says that you should not overcommit cores or vCPUs in VDI, but this is dangerous when using RDS in XenApp.

Some CPUs support hyperthreading. A hyperthread is akin to a logical processor. Hyperthreading takes a hardware thread and multiplies it into two hardware threads. Essentially, what that means is that hyperthreading provides you with the ability to run multiple threads simultaneously as if the CPU had double the cores. Hyperthreading then schedules the instructions to multiple logical processing units. Although logical cores do not perform as well as physical cores, you can still assign hyperthreaded logical cores as if they were physical cores. For example, if you have an eight core processor, you will have 16 logical cores available to assign to your virtual machines. The concept of physical versus virtual cores and hyperthreading is illustrated in the following diagram:

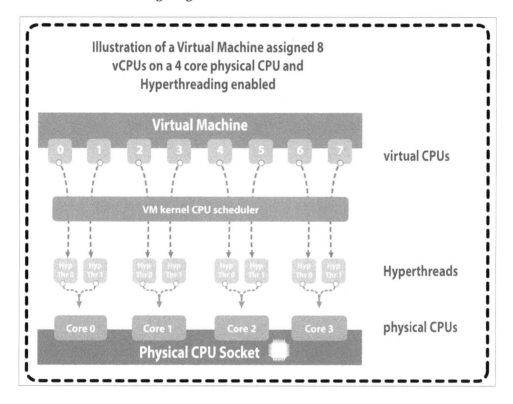

Non-uniform memory access

Non-uniform memory access (**NUMA**) is cache memory for the CPU. NUMA architectures add latency and slow performance. If a VM uses memory that is not part of the same NUMA nodes, it may have performance problems. Most modern hypervisors are NUMA-aware and some allow you to assign NUMA affinity. NUMA architectures use multiple memory buses and attach specific processors to specific high-speed buses connected to specific pools of memory. Memory located in the same NUMA node as the processor is considered local memory and is fast and efficient because it can be accessed quickly. Memory outside of the NUMA node is considered foreign memory and takes longer to access because you have to transfer data outside of the physical CPU to the other physical CPU. NUMA and CPU locality is illustrated in the following diagram. With a NUMA-aware hypervisor, **Virtual Machine 2** should never get assigned to cores across NUMA nodes:

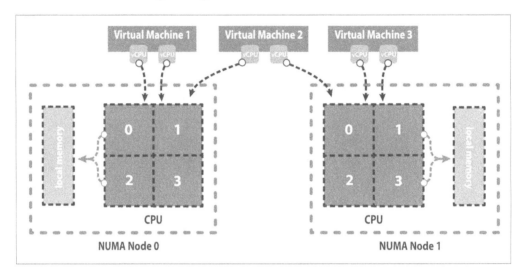

Intel VT

Intel VT represents Intel's technology for virtualization on the x86 platform. Intel VT includes a series of extensions with their existing chipsets for hardware virtualization. VT-x adds migration, priority and memory handling virtualization capabilities to the Intel processors. VT-d adds virtualization support to Intel chipsets that can assign specific I/O devices to specific virtual machines. The VT-c extensions add virtualization support to I/O devices such as network switches.

AMD-V

AMD-V is a set of extensions for the x86 architecture to improve resources and virtual machine performance on the AMD chipsets.

CPU virtualization

CPU virtualization allows you to overcommit CPU resources to virtual machines, which translates into an increase in spare CPU capacity usage. Just about every server you buy these days has support for virtualization, however it still needs to be enabled in the BIOS. CPU virtualization is not the same as CPU emulation. CPU virtualization time-slices physical processors across all virtual machines so that each virtual machine runs as if it had that number of processors allocated to it. A share or slice of each physical processor is allocated to each virtual machine, essentially allowing you to carve up a CPU into multiple CPUs for use across many virtual machines. All virtual machines in the same server are, by default, allocated an equal share of CPU resources. Those shares or slices are referred to as the vCPU.

Hardware-assisted virtualization is most closely aligned with Intel VT and AMD-V virtualization extensions. Hardware-assisted virtualization simply allows a virtual machine to move in and out of different modes of operation. A virtual machine running in a hypervisor is not allowed to access the hardware directly because it is running in user space or guest space. Only the hypervisor can talk directly to the hardware. Hardware-assisted virtualization allows the processor to change state from guest mode into root mode when executing certain operations. When finished, the processor moves the code back to guest mode. Moving into root mode allows the processor to run system calls, traps, page table updates at near native performance which is a performance boost for virtual machines.

> Hardware-assisted virtualization buys you performance in the CPU resources of the server. You must enable it in the server's BIOS.

When you create a virtual machine, you configure it with one or more virtual processors, each with its own set of CPU registers and control structures. When a virtual machine runs, its vCPUs are scheduled to run on physical processors. The hypervisor does the scheduling between virtual and physical CPUs and manages the virtual machine's access to the physical CPU resources.

Today's processors or CPUs have multiple processors embedded in them, called multi-core processors. A single physical CPU that occupies a socket on the computer motherboard might have eight cores. Most motherboards have two sockets. With eight core processors, you would end up with 16 physical cores. With hyperthreading you would have 32 cores (vCPUs) available to assign to VMs. You can also overcommit, meaning you could have more than 32 virtual machines vying for the same vCPUs.

vCPUs assigned to a virtual machine can span different physical cores and sockets. Some hypervisors can determine the relationship between virtual CPUs and socket placement and can maximize performance by keeping vCPUs close to each other for the virtual machines—a process known as CPU affinity. Either way, hypervisors know how to intelligently schedule processing load smoothly across processor cores in the system.

If you want to keep some virtual machines on the same physical processor you can assign CPU affinity, typically in the virtual machine manager. In most cases, you won't need to do this, as the hypervisor will take care of managing the load across all of the processors.

VMware virtual CPUs

The latest VMware ESXi hypervisors don't use emulation, they use hardware-assisted virtualization, taking advantage of the extensions in the Intel VT-x and AMD-V technologies.

The VMware ESXi hypervisor time-slices the physical processors across all virtual machines so that each virtual machine gets a piece of the action. This abstraction is what allows you to assign virtual CPUs to virtual machines. If multiple virtual machines are running, the ESXi hypervisor allocates a share or slice of the physical processors to each virtual machine. If the default resource allocations are used, then all virtual machines get an equal share of resources.

Shares, reservations, and limits

When available resource capacity does not meet the demand of the virtualization overhead and virtual machines, customization of resource allocations is possible in ESXi through the vSphere Web Client.

If a virtual machine is assigned twice as many shares of a resource, such as a vCPU, than another virtual machine, it is entitled to use twice as much of that resource. A reservation guarantees a minimum allocation of a resource, such as a number of vCPUs, per virtual machine. A limit specifies an upper bound for the amount of vCPUs that can be allocated to a virtual machine.

Leaving shares not set gives all VMs equal access to vCPUs. Not setting reservations allows virtual machines to run without requiring a specific vCPU allocation, and vCPU limits default to unlimited. Specifying shares, reservations, and limits might sound like a good idea, but it can end up hindering your virtual machines and waste idle resources by keeping virtual machines within a resource boundary.

When you create a new virtual machine in vSphere Client you can specify the number of vCPUs to allocate to the virtual machine. An example is shown in the following screenshot:

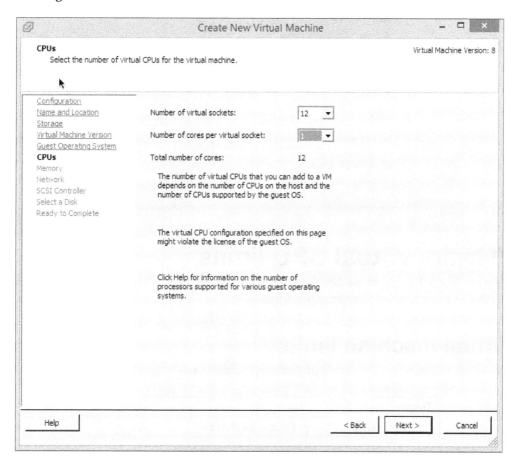

Shares, reservations, and limits can be set for the resource pool in the **Edit Settings** dialog box, as shown in the following screenshot:

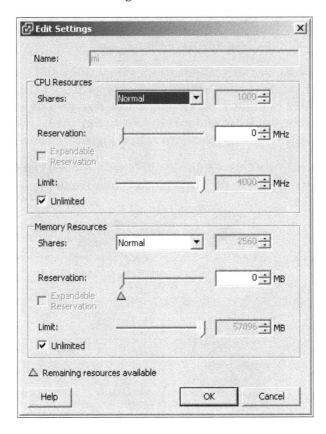

VMware virtual CPU limits

VMware likely has the most developed resources in terms of virtualization software and performance, however, there are limits.

Virtual machine limits

Following table shows the limits of virtual machine on VMware virtual CPU:

Device	Max
Virtual CPUs (vCPUs) per virtual machine	128

VMware ESXi host limits

Following table shows the limits of VMware ESXi host on VMware virtual CPU:

Host CPU	Max
Logical CPUs per host	320
NUMA nodes per socket	16
Virtual machines	**Max**
Virtual machines per host	512
Virtual CPUs per host	4096
Virtual CPUs per core	32

VMware vCPU tweaks

The following tweaks help you tune performance with regards to CPUs in VMware.

Power management

Any form of power management adds latency to a VM. Adjust the BIOS setting for power management to static high so that no OS-controlled power management can engage on the virtual machines. There is a trade off between running cool and lean, so this setting is up to you.

Power settings differ between server manufacturers but you will want to disable power management for C-States, C1E Support, and QPI Power. You will want to enable Turbo Mode or Turbo Boost. You will want to set any power management modes to maximum performance.

NUMA in VMware

NUMA is cache memory for the CPU. NUMA architectures add latency and slow performance. ESXi uses a NUMA-aware scheduler to dynamically balance processor load and memory locality. For best performance, all vCPUs should be scheduled on the same NUMA node and all VM memory should fit and be allocated out of the local physical memory attached to that NUMA node.

Processor affinity for vCPUs on specific NUMA nodes and the VM memory allocated to those NUMA nodes can be set using vSphere Client. However, when you constrain NUMA node affinities, you interfere with the NUMA scheduler to fairly balance the load across NUMA nodes. It is best to leave this setting at the default and let the hypervisor do the scheduling.

Latency sensitivity

In vSphere 5.5, your virtual machines have an option called **Latency Sensitivity** found in the **Advanced Settings** of **VM Options**. Setting this option to **High** will significantly lower latency, jitter, and overhead associated with virtual machine management with regards to the vCPUs, memory, VMXNET3 vNICs and optimized interrupt delivery for VM DirectPath I/O and SR-IOV devices.

XenServer® virtual CPUs

Virtual CPUs in XenServer are similar to vCPUs in VMware. There is a resource sharing algorithm that ensures that virtual machines get their fair share of the host resources, specifically the CPUs.

Assigning a virtual machine's vCPUs to specific physical CPUs in XenServer is referred to as CPU pinning. The vCPU priority weight can be used to grant a virtual machine more CPU time than other virtual machines. The CPU cap fixes the amount of CPU that a virtual machine can use.

As in VMware, changing these values from the defaults isn't really necessary and can actually limit your virtual machines from taking advantage of resource optimizations implemented by the XenServer hypervisor.

XenServer® virtual CPU limits

When configuring vCPU limits on XenServer, please take note of the limits mentioned in the following sections:

Virtual machine limits

Following table shows the limits of virtual machine on XenServer virtual CPU:

Device	Max
Virtual CPUs (vCPUs) per virtual machine (Linux)	32
Virtual CPUs (vCPUs) per virtual machine (Windows)	16

Host limits

Following table shows the limits of host on XenServer virtual CPU:

Host CPU	Max
Logical CPUs per host	160
Concurrent VMs per host (Linux)	650
Concurrent VMs per host (Windows)	500
vGPU VMs per host	96

XenServer® vCPU tweaks

The following tweaks help you tune performance with regards to CPUs in XenServer.

Disable power management

We discussed this in the VMware section and it applies to any hypervisor, including XenServer. Power management options enabled through the BIOS reduce the clock speed on the CPUs. Go into the BIOS and either disable power management or set it to the highest setting for maximum performance. Don't hinder the CPU's you invested all that money in.

Caps, pins, and weights

You can pin VMs to CPUs, give VMs higher weighted priorities for CPU time and cap VMs usage on CPUs. Leave the default settings and let the XenServer hypervisor do the work.

CPU tools

There are some command line tools you can use to check the CPU usage on your XenServer hosts. The tool `host-cpu-tune` can be found in the `/usr/lib/xen/bin/` directory. Other CPU tools include xenpm get-cpu-topology and xl vcpu-list.

irqbalance

One of the CPU hogs can be the processing of interrupts and interrupts queues. The best way to handle this is to use the irqbalance daemon in XenServer. irqbalance keeps all of the IRQ requests from backing up on a single CPU – which would starve resources from your VMs and hinder performance. irqbalance balances interrupt request processing across all Dom0 CPUs. irqbalance is enabled by default.

numad

The **numa daemon** (**numad**) tries to make sure that a process and its memory are in the same numa zone. Using irqbalance and nomad will efficiently balance the load across CPUs without you having to use pinning, weights, or caps.

The number of Dom0 vCPUs

You should have assigned four vCPUs to Dom0. You can find out how many are assigned on each XenServer host by running the command `cat /proc/cpuinfo`. You can find out how load is affecting Dom0 by running the command `xentop` on the Xen console. If Dom0 is over 50% loaded, you can change Dom0 from using four to eight vCPUs. Refer to the article at `http://bit.ly/Dom0vCPUs` for more information.

To set the number of Dom0 vCPUs to eight, use the following command:

```
# NUM=8
# echo "NR_DOMAIN0_VCPUS=${NUM}" > /etc/sysconfig/unplug-vcpus
# /opt/xensource/libexec/xen-cmdline –set-xen dom0_max_vcpus=${NUM}
# reboot
```

Netback threads

If you increase the number of Dom0 vCPUs, you should increase the number of netback threads.

To increase the number of netback threads, use the following code:

```
# vi /boot/extlinux.conf
console=hvc0
xen-netback.netback_max_groups=12
```

Hyper-V virtual CPUs

CPU resources are handled differently in Hyper-V than they are VMware ESXi and XenServer. In VMware and XenServer, if a vCPU slows down, all the other vCPUs will have to slow down, because they are all scheduled or time-sliced together. Microsoft addresses the scheduling problem inside of the guest or virtual machine. As the virtual machine is aware that it is running in a guest within a hypervisor, the operating system knows to schedule processes independently as opposed to combining with vCPU scheduling. Hyper-V understands CPU calls will be coming independently. Oversubscription is not as big of a deal as this method has much less overhead.

A vCPU in Hyper-V is simply a time slice of the physical CPU resource. You can overcommit vCPU resources in Hyper-V as would be expected in any hypervisor. Independent vCPU management is handled automatically by Hyper-V. You can reserve vCPU processing time, assign vCPU processors, and assign weights to vCPU processing priorities in the vCPU settings section for each virtual machine in Hyper-V. Hopefully, by now, you have got the message that you don't need to do this. Use the defaults and let Hyper-V manage the vCPUs.

Hyper-V vCPU limits

When configuring vCPU limits on Hyper-V, take note of the limits mentioned in the following sections:

Virtual machine limits

Following table shows the limits of virtual machine on Hyper-v vCPU:

Device	Max
Virtual CPUs (vCPUs) per virtual machine	64

Host limits

Following table shows the limits of host on Hyper-v vCPU:

Host CPU	Max
Logical CPUs per host	320
Virtual CPUs per server	2048

Hyper-V vCPU tweaks

The following tweaks help you tune performance with regards to CPUs in Hyper-V.

Integration services and Enlightened I/O

There are two things that are absolute musts to get any performance out of Hyper-V. Enable integration services on both the Hyper-V hypervisor (Windows server) and on the virtual machines (Windows 7, 8). This will ensure that the necessary code (the drivers) will be installed into the virtual machine (Windows 7, 8) to allow it take advantage of Hyper-V Enlightened I/O.

Roles

Don't run any other roles on the Windows server. If you need other roles such as DHCP or DNS, run those inside of a virtual machine. Yes, you can run Windows server on a virtual machine on Hyper-V – which runs on Windows server.

64 versus 32

Try to run 64 bit virtual machines. 32 bit operating systems can only address 4 GB of memory, of which, processes can use up to 2 GB.

1:12 overcommit ratio

In Windows Server 2012 R2, Microsoft recommends not overcommitting over the 1:12 ratio of CPU to vCPU.

Summary

Once you understand how virtualization takes up CPU resources and carves them up and distributes their use among many different machines, you come to realize the advantage of virtualization. Just make sure the hypervisor you choose has been built to make the best use of vCPUs and hyperthreading. Virtualization changes everything, including how VMs perform. You need to monitor your hypervisors and VMs to assess how they are performing. In the next chapter, we will discuss monitoring.

8

Performance Monitoring

If you can't see it, you can't manage it. If you can't manage it, you can't monitor it. Why management and monitoring continue to be an afterthought after all of these years, I don't know. There seems to be an obsession with moving data first, then looking at it later. I am not going to go into how to manage XenDesktop, but I will talk about performance monitoring using CLI and GUI tools. Since the usability of XenDesktop is tied directly to performance, you need to understand some of the ways to look at performance to determine if things are running well or if some tweaks need to be made. Following diagram shows an overview of the XenDesktop architecture:

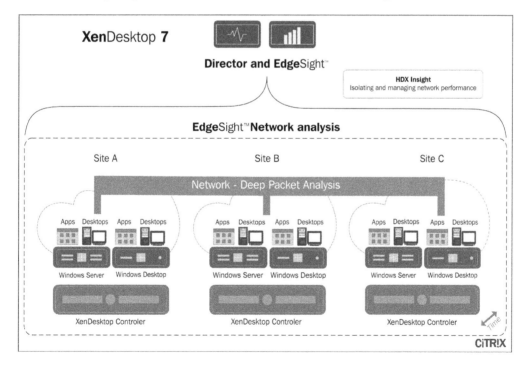

In this chapter, we will cover:

- XenDesktop nugget
- XenDesktop Director
- Citrix HDX insight
- XenDesktop metrics
- Third party tools
- VMware monitoring tools
- Citrix monitoring tools
- Hyper-V monitoring tools
- Load testing

XenDesktop® nugget

I'm convinced XenDesktop is the most powerful VDI solution on the market. I am not completely convinced Citrix has the performance monitoring solution to match. If it was my deployment, I would deploy evaluation versions of most, if not all, of the monitoring tools, and pick and choose which one(s) would work best for the implementation. Some tools require purchasing, others are free and if you are a CLI jockey like me, the free CLI tools are undoubtedly the fastest and most useful.

A key metric that is often looked at in XenDesktop deployments is the ICA **Session Round Trip Time (RTT)** which is an indication of usability. ICA RTT is the time interval measured at the client between the first step (the user action) and the last step (the graphical response displayed). ICA RTT is a good measurement of the screen lag that a user experiences while interacting with the desktop or application. ICA RTT is different from, and always higher than network RTT, which is a measure of network latency. ICA RTT is available via Director, HDX Insight, and EdgeSight and via WMI for third party integrated tools. The best way to determine user experience is to first baseline a single session in secure conditions and also get a baseline of a XenDesktop site under load.

Normal users average in the 100ms range of usability. Users will really start to complain when ICA RTT creeps beyond 1000ms – 2500ms:

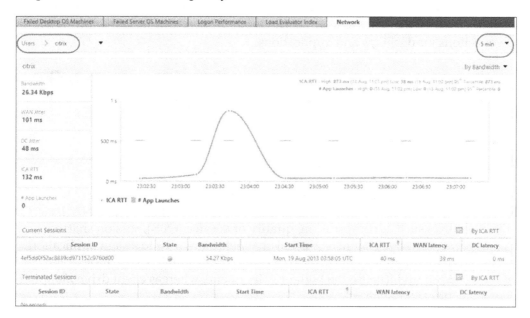

Another indicator of usability is logon time—the amount of time it takes a user to log on to their desktop. What is considered a normal logon time depends on your environment, however, widely accepted logon times have been reported from 10 to 20 seconds:

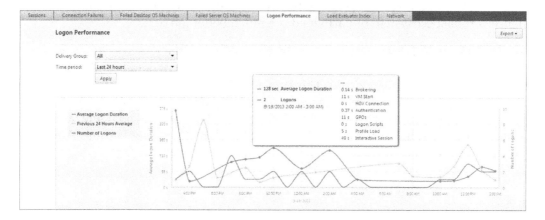

Logon time can be affected by boot storms, that is, the time interval during the day that a massive amount of users try to log on to their desktops at the same time. The XenDesktop site through the Broker Service can control the power state of the machines used by the site. Boot storms can be controlled by setting the throttling of power actions for desktops and applications.

Power actions can be set using the SDK. Refer to the page at `http://bit.ly/XDpwr` for more information.

The ICA protocol

The **Independent Computing Architecture (ICA)** is a proprietary protocol for a desktop or application server designed by Citrix Systems. The ICA protocol has built-in features such as compression, **quality of service (QoS)**, session sharing, keep-alives, and virtual channels. Virtual channels allow you to assign application-specific tasks to different traffic priority queues. For example, video, mouse and keyboard screen updates use the high priority queue, whereas client drive mapping takes a low priority queue.

XenDesktop® Director and EdgeSight®

Back in the Citrix Presentation Server days, Citrix bought a technology called EdgeSight that could monitor user sessions, especially the ICA protocol which is patented by Citrix. EdgeSight was useful, but difficult to implement and use. Hence, a robust ecosystem of partners did a much better job of it.

Any partner could integrate with Citrix by just asking for the ICA specification and signing an NDA. Citrix would hand out the ICA protocol details and APIs to as many partners as they could. This was actually a good thing, because Citrix doesn't do reporting and monitoring very well. Later on there was some angst in business development circles about handing out the ICA protocol so freely, as some competitors ended up with the specification. It didn't really matter because this strategy has served Citrix well.

Citrix later added other features to the protocol and branded them as the **High Definition eXperience (HDX)**, but it is still the same ICA protocol underneath. Also, Citrix realized it wasn't selling enough platinum licenses, so it decided to beef up its monitoring portfolio and introduced a new product called Director.

XenDesktop is monitored with Director. Director is a web-based monitoring tool that ties in nicely with XenDesktop roles which determine what can be displayed. You can view the status of sessions, users, and site infrastructure with XenDesktop Director. You can view users' applications and processes inside of their virtual desktop and quickly help them out by ending unresponsive applications or processes with XenDesktop Director. You can even restart a user's machine for them.

Director is installed by default, as a website, on the XenDesktop delivery controller. You can also install it on a separate server which is actually preferred for a large scale production environment. Following screenshot shows the Director screen:

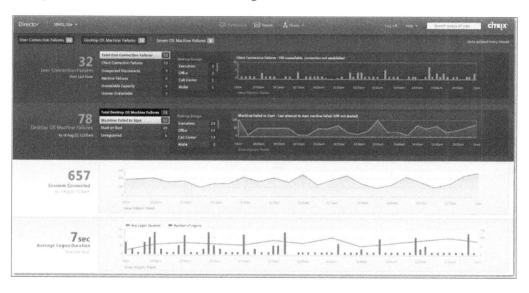

There is a powerful SDK that provides a lot of cmdlets that allow you to manage and monitor the XenDesktop environment. More about the Powershell SDK can be found in my companion book, *Getting Started with XenDesktop® 7.x, Packt Publishing*.

Using HDX Insight™

NetScaler Insight Center is new. It is the EdgeSight network analysis tool and has the EdgeSight performance management functionality integrated with Director. There are two main components of NetScaler Insight Center:

- Web Insight shows performance of web applications

- HDX Insight shows the performance of XenDesktop and XenApp applications

HDX Insight provides application and desktop views of the network. This provides advanced analytics of ICA traffic in the XenDesktop deployment. HDX Insight performance management provides the historical capacity and health trend reporting. A key metric that is often looked at in XenDesktop deployments is the ICA RTT which is an indication of usability.

HDX Insight network analysis must be used with NetScaler Insight Center. NetScaler Insight Center must be installed and configured in Director. NetScaler Insight Center is a virtual machine (appliance) that can be downloaded from `http://citrix.com`. Director gathers information related to XenDesktop from HDX Insight. The analysis it provides is a robust view of the Citrix ICA / HDX protocol from end-to-end from the client all the way through to the back-end infrastructure:

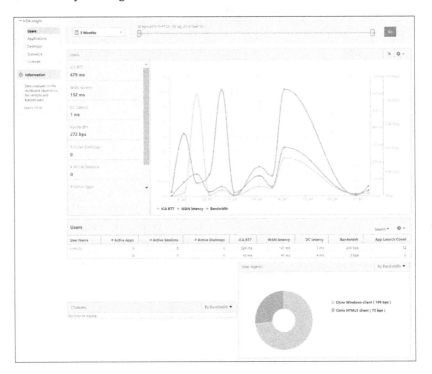

Once you are logged into NetScaler Insight Center and you have added a NetScaler appliance to the inventory, you will see a **Dashboard** tab that shows **Web Insight** and **HDX Insight** data, and another tab called **Configuration** where you add NetScaler and AppFlow connections.

Details on implementing and configuring HDX Insight can be found in my companion book, *Getting Started with XenDesktop® 7.x, Packt Publishing*.

Third-party tools

When it comes to performance monitoring, there is a robust partner ecosystem that Citrix maintains in its Citrix Ready program. Many of these partners have been around since the days when Metaframe became Citrix Presentation Server became XenApp. During the XenApp lifecycle many great third-party tools have been developed. The case can be made that the third-party tools are very robust and, if you can afford it, it's worth looking into these solutions.

eG Innovations

The eG solution works across disparate platforms such as VMware vSphere (ESXi), Citrix XenServer and Microsoft Hyper-V. The nice thing about eG Innovations is that they have solutions for just about every type of application you may be running in your datacenter. When things go south in your XenDesktop site, you will need root-cause analysis fast. eG innovations finds the bottleneck quickly and which resource layer it is in. Whether the pinch point is in storage, networking, CPU, or memory, eG will take you to the solution the fastest.

One of the philosophies of eG is to deploy for performance assurance. In other words, put the performance management tools into place early on in the deployment so you can see how your site performs along every stage from testing the proof of concept to production.

No matter how hard you plan, measure twice and cut once, there will be blind spots in your deployment. It is important to understand usage patterns and how they actually work as against how you thought they would work. eG Innovations has a XenDesktop monitor that helps in the following ways:

- Monitor every layer of the end-to-end XenDesktop deployment
- Visibility into user sessions and applications
- Performance baselining and proactive alerts
- Powerful reporting

[More information can be found at
http://www.eginnovations.com.]

Lakeside software

Lakeside software is another powerful monitoring solution for XenDesktop. Lakeside has a product called SysTrack for XenDesktop.

The best way to see if this will fit your needs is to schedule a demo, which you can do on their website. Lakeside SysTrack has a virtual desktop assessment tool that helps you implement an optimized XenDesktop environment successfully. Lakeside SysTrack can help in the following ways:

- Understand factors that affect user experience
- Quickly diagnose and fix user problems
- Easily execute a pre-virtualization assessment
- Interpret data to improve performance

[More information can be found at
http://www.lakesidesoftware.com.]

There are plenty of solutions to choose from and those worth honorable mention are:

- LiquidWare Labs - http://www.liquidwarelabs.com
- Centrix Software - http://www.centrixsoftware.com
- Goliath Technologies - http://www.goliathtechnologies.com
- Xangati - http://www.xangati.com
- Control UP - http://www.controlup.com
- RES Software – http://www.ressoftware.com
- CA Technologies – http://www.ca.com
- Comtrade – http://www.comtrade.com
- An exhaustive list can be found on the Citrix Ready website at http://www.citrixready.citrix.com/ready

XenDesktop® performance metrics

There are a few performance metrics that are worth monitoring in your XenDesktop environment. These metrics apply to the Windows virtual machines. They are listed here in the following table:

Metric	Descripton
Processor - % processor time	The percentage of time it takes to execute a thread. Calculated by observing the time the service is inactive and subtracting it from 100%. It depends on the process, but up to 70%-80% might be acceptable for one process.
System – processor queue length	The number of threads in the processor queue. This shows threads that are ready to run, not threads that are already running. A long CPU queue is a symptom of a CPU bottleneck. Up to five threads per core for five minutes is acceptable.
Memory – available bytes	The amount of memory available after non-paged pool allocations. If you get down to only 30% memory available, you should keep an eye on this.
Memory – pages / sec	The rate at which pages are read from or written to disk from memory. A high value indicates a memory bottleneck or a program accessing a lot of memory.
Paging File - % usage	The percentage amount of the page file instance in use. Up to 40% is considered acceptable.
Logical Disk / Physical Disk - % Free Space	The percentage of total usable free space on the logical disk that is free. Less than 10% free space is getting close to uncomfortable.
Logical Disk / Physical Disk - % Disk Time	The percentage of time the disk is busy. Anything over 70% is considered uncomfortable.
Logical Disk / Physical Disk – Current Disk Queue Length	The number of transactions waiting to be processed to disk. A long disk queue indicates a storage bottleneck. Monitor available memory also. This is where you will see excessive IOPS.
Logical Disk / Physical Disk – Avg Disk Sec / Read - Avg Disk Sec / Write - Avg Disk Sec / Transfer	The average time in seconds for read, write, and transfers from/to a disk. High latency indicates a storage bottleneck. Times should be in the range below 15 ms.

Metric	Descripton
Network Interface – bytes / sec	The rate at which the network adapters are processing bytes. High values could indicate a network bottleneck.
Database Avg Transaction Time	The time it takes to execute a database transaction. A high value could indicate a bottleneck with SQL Server.
Database Connected	Indicates whether XenDesktop is in contact with its SQL database.
Database Transaction Errors / sec	The rate at which database transactions are failing. High values indicate an issue with the SQL database.

VMware monitoring tools

When monitoring XenDesktop on VMware, take note of the tools mentioned in the following sections:

GUI tools

VMware undoubtedly has the largest array of management products. vSphere Client and vSphere Web Client allow you to connect to a vCenter Server. XenDesktop requires vCenter, so with any proof of concept or deployment you will need vCenter. vSphere Client and vSphere Web Client need to run on a Windows OS on either a physical or virtual machine. vCenter can also run on a physical or virtual machine within ESXi.

The vSphere Client and vSphere Web Client along with vCenter provide some basic monitoring information for memory, CPU, network, and storage of virtual machines.

CLI tools

vSphere supports several command-line interfaces for managing your virtual infrastructure including the **vSphere Command-Line Interface (vCLI)**, a set of ESXi shell commands, and PowerCLI. You can choose the CLI set best suited for your needs, and write scripts to automate your CLI tasks.

vCLI

The vCLI command can be run from any type of system, you just need to install the package. You run these commands remotely against a target ESXi server.

PowerCLI

vSphere 5.5 includes a PowerCLI tool. vCLI provides a Windows PowerShell interface to the vSphere API, which includes over 200 cmdlets, simple scripts and a function library for automation and management.

There is far more information about PowerCLI than can be covered in this book. However some of the PowerCLI cmdlets you should look into are the following:

PowerCLI cmdlet	Description
Get-VM	This cmdlet retrieves a list of virtual machines from the vCenter server
Get-EsxTop	This cmdlet exposes the esxtop functionality. Esxtop provides a valuable monitoring insight into counters for ESXi hosts and virtual machines

esxtop

VMware provides a CLI tool called esxtop that provides a real-time view of ESXi. This handy little tool has been around for a long time and provides insight into just about every part of the system you need to look at such as the network, computing, storage, and memory.

esxtop is a CLI tool, so you will need to log in to the ESXi hypervisor console using ssh.

Once you are inside of the esxtop utility, you can change between the different metrics by typing in characters on the keyboard. The following keys and their associated views are represented in the following table:

esxtop keyboard key	Description
m	Memory
c	CPU
n	Network
d	Disk adapter
u	Disk device
v	Disk VM
i	Interrupts
p	Power states

esxtop keyboard key	Description
f	Add/remove fields
V	Show only virtual machine stats
s X	Refresh the screen every x seconds
spacebar	Refresh screen

Memory

The following metrics are of particular value in esxtop when monitoring the memory:

Metric	Description
MCTLSZ (MB)	The amount of virtual machine physical memory (MB) the ESXi hypervisor is reclaiming through the balloon driver. This is an indicator of memory overcommitment.
MEM overcommit	Indicates memory overcommitment for the last one, five and fifteen minutes.
VMKMEM (MB) high state	There is enough free memory available.
VMKMEM (MB) soft state	Hypervisor is reclaiming memory through the balloon driver.
VMKMEM (MB) hard state	Hypervisor is swapping memory. This is an indicator of performance issues.
VMKMEM (MB) low state	Hypervisor will stop VMs to allocate more memory. You don't want to be in this state.
SWCUR (MB)	Memory that has been swapped by the hypervisor.
ZIP (sec), UNZIP (sec)	Hypervisor is compressing (ZIP) or de-compressing (UNZIP) memory.
CACHEUSD (MB)	Cached memory by the hypervisor
SWR (sec), SWW (sec)	The rate at which the hypervisor is reading from or writing to swapped memory. Another indicator of overcommitment.
NMN	NUMA Node (CPU Cache) the VM is using
N%L	Percentage of memory at the local NUMA Node. High values are good.
NRMEM (MB)	Amount of memory at the remote NUMA node. High values are bad.
NLMEM	Amount of memory at the local NUMA node. High values are good.

CPU

The following metrics are of particular value in esxtop when monitoring the CPU:

Metric	Description
%USED	CPU Core cycles used by a VM. High values indicate a performance problem
CPU Load	The CPU load average for the last one, five, and fifteen minutes
%SYS	Indicates percentage of time processing interrupts
%VMWAIT	Indicates percentage of time a VM is waiting for the hypervisor to complete an activity
%SWPWT	Indicates percentage of time a VM is waiting for swapped pages to be read from disk
%WAIT	Indicates percentage of time a VM is idle
%RDY	Indicates percentage of time a VM is waiting to be scheduled
%MLMTD	Indicates percentage of time not scheduled

Network

The following metrics are of particular value in esxtop when monitoring the network:

Metric	Description
%DRPTX	Indicates % of dropped packets – on transmit
%DRPRX	Indicates % of dropped packets – on receive
Used-by/TEAM-PNIC	Tells you which NIC the VM is using

Storage

The following metrics are of particular value in esxtop when monitoring the storage:

Metric	Description
DAVG	Latency at the device driver level
ABRTS (sec)	Commands aborted per second. Aborts indicate longer than 60 second wait times from VM to storage data transfers
KAVG	Latency in the VMkernel or hypervisor. High values indicate queueing issues
GAVG	Latency for the group = KAVG + DAVG
Resets (sec)	The number of command resets per second

XenServer® monitoring tools

When monitoring XenDesktop on XenServer, take note of the tools mentioned in the following sections:

GUI tools

XenCenter is the GUI application that is used to manage and monitor XenServer. XenCenter runs on a Windows OS either on a physical or virtual machine. Not only is this an easy to use interface for creating resources, it contains valuable metrics for performance management, including some easy to read graphs. Complete details on XenCenter performance graphs can be found in the XenCenter Help. The metrics available in XenCenter provide valuable insight into memory CPU, network, and storage performance:

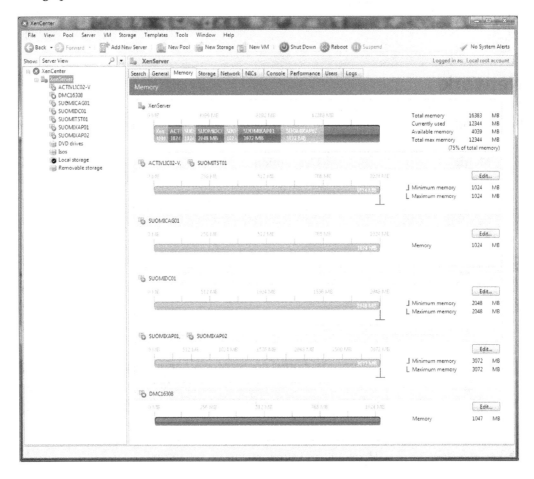

CLI tools

When monitoring XenDesktop on XenServer, take note of the following CLI tools.

Round Robin Databases

XenServer uses **Round Robin Databases (RRDs)** to store performance metrics which consist of multiple **Round Robin Archives (RRAs)** — circular buffers with predefined capacity.

> More information on RRDs can be found at `http://bit.ly/xenrrds`.

A complete list of available metrics for the XenServer hypervisor host along with the virtual machines is available in the XenServer Administrators Guide in *Chapter 9, Acceleration*.

> The XenServer 6.5 Administration Guide can be downloaded from `http://bit.ly/xen6-5`.

xentop

XenServer also provides a CLI tool called xentop that provides a real-time view of XenServer. This tool also provides insight into every part of the system you need to look at, such as the network, computing, storage, and memory. xentop reports on Dom0 along with all of the other virtual machines running in user space.

xentop is a CLI tool, so you will need to log in to the XenServer hypervisor console using ssh.

Before we talk about the hardware stack, there are several states a virtual machine can be in, as reported by the statemetric. The following table illustrates those potential states:

xentop States	Description
d	The domain is dying
s	The domain is shutting down
b	The domain is blocked

xentop States	Description
c	The domain has crashed
p	The domain is paused
r	The domain is actively running

Memory

The following metrics are displayed in column format in xentop when monitoring the memory:

Metric	Description
MEM (k)	Displays current memory
MAXMEM (k)	Displays maximum domain memory statistics in KB
MAXMEM (%)	Displays memory in a ratio of current domain memory to total node memory

CPU

The following metrics are displayed in column format in xentop when monitoring the CPU:

Metric	Description
CPU (sec)	Displays CPU usage in seconds for that virtual machine
CPU (%)	Displays CPU usage as a percentage for that virtual machine
VCPUS	Displays the number of virtual CPUs for that virtual machine

Network

The following metrics are displayed in column format in xentop when monitoring the network:

Metric	Description
NETTX (k)	Displays the total number of bytes transmitted / 1024
NETRX (k)	Displays the total number of bytes received / 1024

Storage

The following metrics are displayed in column format in xentop when monitoring storage:

Metric	Description
VBDS	Displays the number of virtual block devices
VBD OO	Displays the number of out of request errors resulting in I/O operations
VBD RD	Displays the number of read requests
VBD WR	Displays the number of write requests

xenmon

Another tool in XenServer called xenmon can help you focus in on which domains are using the most CPU. xenmon displays reports for each CPU and defaults to CPU 0. To view the other CPUs, press the *p* and *n* keys to page through each CPU.

xm

Another tool that is useful for looking at virtual machines is a tool called xm. In addition to other performance tools, xm can be used to start and shutdown virtual machines. xm can also be used to list information about virtual machines by using xm info and xm list.

Hyper-V monitoring tools

When monitoring XenDesktop on Hyper-V, take note of the tools mentioned in the following sections.

GUI tools

When monitoring XenDesktop on Hyper-V, take note of the following GUI tools.

Hyper-V Manager

Hyper-V in Windows Server 2012 R2 can be managed and monitored with Hyper-V Manager GUI through the **Remote Server Administration Tools** (**RSAT**) on a Windows desktop such as Windows 8.1. Hyper-V on Windows Server 2008 R2 can be managed with Hyper-V Manager on Windows 7.

XenDesktop connects to Hyper-V through Microsoft **System Center Virtual Machine Manager (SCVMM)**, and with SCVMM you can do some management of Hyper-V as well.

Another GUI tool worth presenting is the Failover Cluster Manager. Hyper-V differs from the VMware and XenServer hypervisors in that virtual machines are considered to be objects in one console, clustered resources in the next, and just virtual machines in the third console.

You access Hyper-V Manager through an MMC plug-in. Click on **Start | Run | ServerManager.msc | Expand Roles | Hyper-V**.

CLI tools

When monitoring XenDesktop on Hyper-V, take a note of the CLI tools mentioned in the following sections.

PowerShell library

As you know, Hyper-V runs as a service on top of Microsoft Windows Server. There are some useful CLI tools available for monitoring Hyper-V through the PowerShell API.

 To enable and access PowerShell on the Hyper-V host, refer to my companion book, *Getting Started with XenDesktop® 7.x, Packt Publishing*.

Resource metering

Windows Server 2012 R2 Hyper-V includes a resource metering mechanism that makes it possible to track system resources for virtual machines. It is not enabled by default, so you will need to enable it by opening the PowerShell window and entering the following command:

```
# Get-VM <virtual machine name> | Enable-VMResourceMetering
```

With resource metering enabled, you can view the metric data for one or all of the virtual machines. To view metrics for a single virtual machine, open a PowerShell window and enter the following command:

```
# Get-VM <virtual machine name> | Measure-VM
```

To view metrics for all virtual machines, open a PowerShell window, and enter the following command:

```
# Get-VM | Measure-VM
```

To display metrics for a specific metering object, you need to get a list of those objects. This can be done by entering the following command:

```
# Get-VM | Measure-VM | Select-Object *
```

After reviewing the metering objects that are available, you can focus in on them by specifying them in the command line:

```
# Get-VM | Measure-VM | Select-Object VMName, MaxRAM
```

Memory

The following metrics can be viewed in Hyper-V with the Get-VM | Measure-VM resource metering command for monitoring memory for virtual machines:

Metric	Description
AvgRAM(M)	Displays average physical memory usage
MaxRAM(M)	Displays maximum physical memory usage
MinRAM(M)	Displays minimum physical memory usage

CPU

The following metrics can be viewed in Hyper-V with the Get-VM | Measure-VM resource metering command for monitoring the CPU for virtual machines:

Metric	Description
AvgCPU(Mhz)	Displays average CPU usage in Megahertz

Network

The following metrics can be viewed in Hyper-V with the Get-VM | Measure-VM resource metering command for monitoring the network for virtual machines:

Metric	Description
NetworkInbound(M)	Displays inbound Megabytes for the virtual network adapter
NetworkOutbound(M)	Displays outbound Megabytes for the virtual network adapter

Storage

The following metrics can be viewed in Hyper-V with the `Get-VM | Measure-VM` resource metering command for monitoring the storage for virtual machines:

Metric	Description
`TotalDisk(M)`	Displays the total amount of disk space allocated to the virtual machine

Load testing

Login VSI is really the only company out there that effectively performs load testing on a VDI infrastructure.

 More information on Login VSI can be found at http://www.loginvsi.com.

Login VSI was a bit difficult to use in the early versions, but they tout that the latest versions are easier to use than before. If you have ever read a performance report about Virtual Desktop Infrastructure, then Login VSI was likely the basis for that testing. If you are implementing a small-to-medium deployment of VDI, the risk of finding and mitigating performance issues is the same as it would be for a large deployment.

The reality is, no matter how much time and preparation you put into making sure your solution is built for performance, there is always a chance some hidden issues will pop up just when you are ready to launch into production.

There are many white papers and how-tos for Login VSI out there if you search for them. Login VSI allows you to use built-in workloads or customize your own. They also produce a VSImax metric that can be used to establish a baseline of "how much" and "how big" you can safely run your VDI deployment into the thousands of users.

There are other tools out there to do some performance testing if you search for them. Some of these tools are listed here:

- Goliath
- LoadGen by Denamik
- Bonnie++
- Iozone

- Storm VM
- VMTurbo
- Zenpack for XenServer
- Verax Systems
- Op5
- LogicMonitor
- HypOps
- Hotlink

However, to effectively test VDI, you need a tool that can launch the desktop and run applications from desktops to emulate load.

Summary

Monitoring is critical to the performance of your VDI deployment. Even if you don't have performance issues at the start, you should put together a list of metrics and a methodology for monitoring those metrics. A baseline measurement should be taken to give you an idea of how VDI looks when it is running smoothly with plenty of breathing room. You will then know when performance issues start to develop and you can get out in front of them. In this chapter, you learned about many different methods for monitoring XenDesktop.

To briefly summarize the steps required to monitor a XenDesktop site, you can use the following:

- Complete the XenDesktop deployment
- Build and test with a load simulator such as Login VSI
- Monitor and interpret the results
- Tweak and tune the environment
- Ongoing measurement to identify performance issues

In the next chapter we will discuss the concepts of accelerating the XenDesktop infrastructure.

9
Acceleration

You can control performance inside the hypervisors, hardware, and the datacenter in which you deploy your XenDesktop infrastructure. You cannot control performance outside of these, but there are things you can do to help improve performance beyond the XenDesktop site.

In this chapter, we will cover the following:

- XenDesktop nugget
- Application Delivery Controllers
- WAN optimization
- Content Delivery Networks
- 3D, HD, and HDX
- Thin clients

XenDesktop® nugget

Communication from the XenDesktop site to the client or end user happens over the ICA/HDX protocol. ICA/HDX runs over TCP, and, with the recent acquisition of Framehawk, can now use UDP. You can't really control what happens on the Internet with regard to performance. You can install tools to speed things up, however, and these are within your sphere of control. Implementing a NetScaler **Application Delivery Controller** (**ADC**) and CloudBridge WAN optimization can improve performance significantly for certain environments. Both NetScaler and CloudBridge optimize ICA/HDX.

An ADC might get you a improvement in performance of more than 5%. A WAN Optimization Controller might get you a improvement in performance of more than 90%. Using a **Content Delivery Network** (**CDN**) can improve performance from 20% to more than 100%.

The real benefit of an ADC in front of a XenDesktop site is the SSL security that encrypts the communication. Load balancing may help improve performance in large deployments for more than 10,000 users, but it is more about providing high availability and Citrix prefers that you use NetScaler as the load balancer, although it is not required.

Application Delivery Controllers

An ADC is an appliance in a datacenter that sits in front of servers to offload the heavy lifting of performance-related tasks. I talk about ADCs in my companion book, *Getting Started with XenDesktop® 7.x, Packt Publishing*. If you refer back to *Chapter 1, XenDesktop® Architecture*, in this book, and look at the network diagram, you can see Citrix NetScaler as the frontend to the XenDesktop site.

There are many vendors that supply ADC besides providing SSL to your clients. ADCs are generally a good piece of equipment when it comes to load balancing, caching, compression, and high availability.

Load balancer

A load balancer is a device that acts as a reverse proxy and distributes network and application traffic across a number of servers. A side benefit is that they provide high availability, because, if a server goes down or malfunctions, the load balancer elegantly load balances around it so that no user ever has to encounter a service interruption. The main component of a load balancer is the TCP multiplexing ratio, which is the number of incoming TCP connections from the clients to the number of outbound TCP connections to the backend servers. Depending on the workload you can get anywhere from 10:1 to 1000:1 ratios.

Load balancers from other vendors could potentially be used to load balance servers in the XenDesktop architecture. There are even some free and open source load balancers out there if you search for them. Again, you may not see a significant performance improvement unless you have a very large deployment of 10,000 users or more.

Secure ticket authority

Citrix prefers that the NetScaler be the only frontend to the XenDesktop site through the interaction with the **secure ticket authority (STA)** parameter. In some ways it ensures that NetScaler will be the only available frontend you can use in front of XenDesktop if accessing the XenDesktop site without a VPN. However, other load balancers such as F5 Big-IP can be used as well.

ADC caching

Caching is a feature of an ADC that stores recently used information from backend servers such as text, HTML, images, and scripts. In the old days, caching was performed by the web servers themselves. ADCs have evolved to offload this function from the web server so they can do what they do best—serve content. Caching is part of the HTTP Internet RFC specification.

ADC compression

Compression is a feature of ADCs that compresses content to make it smaller, therefore reducing the amount of information that has to be sent from the datacenter to the client, which speeds up performance. Compression is part of the HTTP Internet RFC specification. Compression from an ADC perspective means that any content that is compressible can be compressed and you can specify exactly which objects you want to apply compression to. However, compression at the ADC, as you might discover, is limited to objects that are compressible, and there aren't that many in a XenDesktop infrastructure. In some cases, trying to compress objects that are already compressed, such as images, videos, and PDFs, causes an added performance hit by trying to compress something twice, which is an unneeded burn of cycles.

WAN Optimization Controllers

The real benefit in performance from datacenter to client comes in the **WAN Optimization Controller** (**WOC**). A WOC is an appliance that employs a collection of technologies to increase data transfer performance across a WAN. A WAN is any network that data has to cross to get from the datacenter to the end user or client. The most common WANs that you will run into are the Internet (public) and leased lines (private). The physical infrastructure that makes up these networks is a long list of optical dark fibers (underground) and copper (above ground). In some remote locations you might find DSL, cable, or even satellite. One thing is for sure, the connection from your datacenter to the client and everything in between will not be made of the same type. All of the different types of networks mean there will be latency. You have no control over the network, but you do have the means to overcome the latency. When you encounter latency greater than 100 to 200 ms between endpoints, the best way to speed that up is by using WAN optimization.

WAN caching

Caching is a part of the HTTP Internet Engineering Task Force Draft Specification. However, caching doesn't apply only to HTTP Internet traffic. Caching is an area of a computer's memory or disk dedicated to storing commonly used information. The degree of performance improvement depends on how close the cache device is to the user. WOCs and CDNs get the cache closest to the user, so the improvement is astounding. ADCs are capable of caching, but they reside in the datacenter, far away from the end user, so the performance improvement is lower. Most often a WOC or CDN uses an OEMed server that uses memory and disk to cache the data.

The way this works is that data is sent from the point of origin, such as a datacenter, and cached at the other end, close to the client. When a client requests that data, it is served from the local cache as opposed to being served from the origin server across the network, removing the chance that the transfer will incur latency caused by the long trip of the WAN.

WAN compression

Compression is also a part of the HTTP Internet Engineering Task Force Draft Specification. Data compression has been used in web browsers and HTTP servers for a long time. Compression enables two technology endpoints to transmit or store data in a smaller number of bits than the original data.

The way this works is that data is compressed at the point of origin and decompressed at the other end, close to the client.

WAN de-duplication

Data de-duplication is a technique for eliminating duplicates and repeating data patterns. It is extremely effective on whitespace.

The way this works is that data is parsed by the de-dup mechanism. Any duplicates or repeating patterns of data are replaced with a byte sequence. This significantly reduces the amount of data that needs to be transmitted. When the data arrives at the other end, the duplicate data or repeating patterns are re-inserted to form the original data stream.

WAN latency reduction

Many filesystem protocols were not designed to work over long distances such as WANs. Latency reduction is the art of re-engineering filesystem protocols to remove the inefficiencies that cause latency. For example, CIFS is a very chatty protocol requiring responses from the client to the server before more data can be sent. WOCs deal with this by buffering data and removing the extra receipt/response mechanism from the protocol. The chatty-ness is then reduced and handled locally between the WOC-server and WOC-client, thus removing the latency caused by the protocol.

Some WOCs simply perform this by forcing the WOCs to communicate with each other using hard and fast connection parameters, ignoring the handshaking protocols used in the WAN.

WAN quality of service

Quality of service is a method of marking certain packets to be sent first at a higher priority than other packets, thusnsuring fast delivery. Some WOCs allow you to set some quality of service parameters for your traffic.

WAN protocol optimization

Many protocols, such as TCP, are not optimized by design. Protocol optimization is the art of re-engineering the transports protocol and replacing the inefficient methods with efficient methods of transfer. There have been a few improvements and revisions to the TCP protocol to remove inefficiencies, such as TCP Reno and Fast TCP. Although these improvements have been engineered, the majority of links use legacy implementations. To take advantage of faster TCP methods you may need to insert some WOCs into your network or use a network that has Fast TCP methods built in.

Content Delivery Networks

A **Content Delivery Network (CDN)** is a large distributed system of servers deployed in multiple data centers across the globe. A CDN is the ultimate tool for acceleration as it enjoys the greatest speeds when it comes to accelerating data. You can think of a CDN as a service that you pay for, and the vendor provides and manages the acceleration appliances. You don't have to do anything except pay for the service, so no talent and skillsets are needed on your team. In addition, CDNs have hundreds, if not thousands, of appliances (similar to WOCs) in datacenters all over the world, so the service is already as close to the end user as it needs to be. CDNs implement all of the same features of an ADC and WOC and they do it on a global scale.

The organization that invented the CDN back in 1998 is Akamai. They have the largest market share and undoubtedly the largest number of enterprise customers that rely on their CDN provide the best user experience. Not only do they have the largest managed CDN with 170,000 servers around the world, but they also have products that you can buy to build your own CDN—although I'm not sure why you would want to do that unless you were a service provider.

Akamai is a partner of Citrix although CDNs are a bit of a competitor to the ADC and WOC. If you lease a CDN service, it doesn't make sense to buy expensive ADC and WOC technology. If you lease a CDN service, the only real benefit you would get out of an ADC is the SSL security and the load balancing of your XenDesktop servers, if implementing a large deployment.

Virtual Desktop Infrastructure Content Delivery Network

A **Virtual Desktop Infrastructure Content Delivery Network (VDI CDN)** is a virtual desktop infrastructure that leverages the power of the CDN. This is a new concept to the world of VDI. In VDI, the user's virtual desktop runs on the XenDesktop infrastructure and the visual pieces are just bits of JPEG images sent and refreshed across a large keyboard-video-mouse connection. It makes sense to cache those images closer to the end user in a CDN, especially if you are running a large scale deployment of VDI.

The CDN would essentially plug into the network cloud if referring to the XenDesktop architecture diagram discussed in *Chapter 1, XenDesktop® Architecture*. Putting a CDN in between your clients and the XenDesktop site would complicate matters, so it's important to do a proof of concept.

Three dimensional graphics and high definition

Rich multi-dimensional graphics are here to stay. **Three dimensional (3D)**graphics are computer-generated graphics that use a three-dimensional representation of geometric data. **High definition (HD)** is a relatively new term in computer display technology that proposes to display HD video on computer screens. Familiar screen resolutions for HD are 720p and 1080p. 720p and 1080p refer to the width of the screen in pixels. This follows a similar display geometry that the television industry is embarking on. The reason that HD in computer displays are aligning with HD in television displays is video.

HDX in the television industry is simply HD pixel formats encoded at high bitrates for even crisper visual and audio effects. Citrix also came up with the term HDX to embody a rich high definition user experience. HDX is covered in my companion book, *Getting Started with XenDesktop® 7.x, Packt Publishing*.

The further up the high definition experience and 3D scale you go, the more performance is required to make it happen all around, from client to server.

HDX™

Real-time multimedia transcoding enables audio and video media streaming to mobile devices, and by improving how Windows media content is delivered over a WAN, it enhances the user experience. There are a couple of important terms used here. Transcoding transforms the media content from one encoding format to another. For example, this means compressing media to reduce the file size or converting data to a format supported on the target device. Transrating alters the bit rate of the media based on network conditions; for example, by decreasing the media's resolution or frame rate to achieve a lower bit rate.

When this feature is enabled, real-time multimedia transcoding is deployed automatically to enable media streaming, which provides a seamless user experience even in extreme network conditions. Transcoding occurs on the **Virtual Delivery Agent** (**VDA**) for the virtual desktop. If the DA has a supported GPU for hardware acceleration, transcoding is done in the GPU. Otherwise, it is performed in the server's CPU. The media is then trans-rated to achieve the target transmission bit rate and redirected to the client device, where it is decompressed and rendered.

The important distinction is in where the transcoding and trans-rating is being processed, on the client device or the XenDesktop host that is running the virtual desktop. Since 3D and high definition graphics require intensive computational resources, it becomes a matter of performance importance.

If your client device has the power of a workstation with a good graphics chipset, then some graphics will be rendered there. If your client device has the power of a smartphone or low end thin client, then the graphics will be rendered in the server. Who has the most power, the client or the server — that will tell you where the graphics will be churned and crunched before being displayed on the user's device.

If you are going to support a high definition experience in virtualized environments, you are going to need the server hardware with enough power to deliver it.

HDX™ 3D

HDX 3D enables you to serve desktops and applications that require a dedicated GPU for hardware acceleration. HDX 3D is suitable for use with DirectX and OpenGL-driven applications, and with rich media videos.

A small subset of the market is virtualizing their 3D applications. What these 3D customers and vendors are finding is that, even though their solutions are very costly, they can still save some money with HDX. Running a 3D application on a server and delivering it to a virtual desktop and then out to a client requires the presence of a high-performance 3D video card on the server that is running the VDA.

NVidia owns this market with their NVidia GRID vGPU technology that enables hardware virtualization of the GPU. The NVidia GRID vGPU technology is compatible with most, if not all, server hardware platforms: Dell, HP, IBM, and SuperMicro. The NVidia GRID vGPU technology is compatible with all major hypervisors such as VMware ESXi, Citrix XenServer, and Microsoft Hyper-V.

When it comes to GPUs and XenDesktop, there are different usage models, discussed at `http://bit.ly/xdgpus` and `http://bit.ly.xdgpus2`.

If you are going to support 3D applications in virtualized environments, there is no question that you will need a server that has multiple NVidia cards. Note that one desktop does not fit all, and in the FlexCast model, it would be easier to deliver standard desktops and supplement these with graphics desktops as needed. One NVidia Kepler card can be shared with many VMs.

Thin clients

As covered in my companion book, *Getting Started with XenDesktop® 7.x*, *Packt Publishing*, many thin client vendors are integrating with Citrix Receiver to provide a seamless experience with virtual desktops delivered by XenDesktop. Some thin client models have a thin OS, usually a flavor of Linux, with the Citrix Receiver code built in, so that it can connect to the virtual desktop quickly and automatically. Other models have the Windows operating system running with Citrix Receiver.

They key to performance when using thin clients is to make sure they have enough power. Many thin client vendors really ratchet down the cost of the **bill Of materials** (**BOM**) by using low end components and processors. Lower cost means lower performance.

If you are considering using thin clients to run the virtual desktop for your users, do yourself a favor and read the reviews. More importantly, do a proof of concept with as many thin clients as you can, because the proof is in the actual performance you can see happening before your eyes. There are many thin client vendors that claim high performance in a small, compact, low-cost device, but they don't perform at minimum levels when you get them plugged in.

Summary

Acceleration is something that you should not overlook, at least in the planning stages. There are tools to help reduce latency and improve the user experience, so do yourself a favour and at least investigate the cost versus benefit of using them. In the next chapter, we will discuss some additional performance tweaks for XenDesktop components.

10
XenDesktop® Component Tweaks

Now that you understand every piece of the VDI infrastructure from client to server, you can focus on picking out which performance tweaks apply to you and putting together a list of the ones you want to implement. Perfect performance and usability do not happen by default, you have to make it happen. We have covered some performance enhancing tweaks in earlier chapters. In this chapter we will cover some additional performance enhancing tweaks for individual VDI components.

In this chapter, we will cover performance tweaks for:

- Citrix Receiver
- Virtual desktops
- StoreFront
- Studio
- Director
- Delivery Controller
- License Server
- Active Directory
- DHCP and DNS
- SQL databases
- Provisioning server

 Always make backups of your files before making any changes. Have a rollback plan, even if it is as simple as making a copy of a file to a backup file.

Citrix Receiver™ tweaks

In most cases, you will not need to tweak the Citrix Receiver application on the end user device. In the rare instances that your end user happens to be on the other side of the globe using international connections, using satellite or on an oil-rig platform at sea, then you might want to consider these. In other words, if the network latency between the end user and the XenDesktop datacenter is greater than 200 ms, then you have a case for tweaks. Otherwise, leave the defaults.

Configuring Citrix Receiver will take some research. Some tweaks can be done with GPOs while others can be done with registry settings. Citrix doesn't put those into one nice easy place to get to or manage. You may have to search for them, but some of that is done for you at.

Caching

Bitmap caching stores commonly used images on the client's local disk. If you have a high speed LAN, you don't need to use the following parameter:

Parameter	Description	Default setting
PersistentCacheEnabled	Bitmap caching stores commonly used images on the local disk	Off
PersistentCacheMinBitmap	The size of the smallest bitmap to cache in KB	8
PersistentCacheSize	The size of the cache in MB	10

Compression

Compression reduces the amount of data you have to send over the network. On limited bandwidth or high latency networks, more compression is better. However, if you don't have latency issues, higher compression takes up more computing power, so it is a trade off. Keep in mind that every tweak comes with a cost, by delivering a slightly less than optimal experience for the user with regards to quality. Following are its parameters:

Parameter	Description	Default setting
Compress	Sets default data compression	On
MaximumCompression	Turn on for high compression, turn off for normal compression	Off

Keyboard and mouse

You have heard me say that from the Citrix Receiver to the XenDesktop site is just a long **keyboard, video, and mouse (KVM)** cable sending key strokes, bitmaps, and mouse commands over the network. Following are its parameters:

Parameter	Description	Default setting
MouseTimer	The time in milliseconds between mouse movement updates sent to the server. 0 disables this. Enable it for high latency networks.	0
ZLKeyboardMode	Speedscreen latency reduction mode. 0 (off) 1 (on) 2 (auto). Only use on high latency networks.	0
ZLMouseMode	Speedscreen latency reduction mode. 0 (off) 1 (on) 2 (auto). Only use on high latency networks.	2

Citrix® Virtual Desktop tweaks

There are some performance tweaks you can perform on the virtual desktop. There are a couple of ways to do this, but it has to be done on the master image. The two methods are:

- Select the option to optimize the desktop when you install the Virtual Delivery Agent
- Run the TargetOSOptimizer tool manually on the master image

> Running the optimizer can take a long time and you need to let it finish. A backup file called optimizations.reg is stored in the installation folder c:\Program Files (x86)\Citrix\TargetOSOptimizer that reverts the registry settings.

The optimizer disables certain functions of the virtual desktop that could impact performance such as disabling autoupdate, offline files, disk defragmentation, background layout service, system restore, last access time stamp, hibernate mode, crashdump, indexing, clear page file, superfetch, defender, and search. It also reduces the IE temporary cache file size and event log size.

Tribal Knowledge says that more performance tweaks can be found for virtual desktops at `http://bit.ly/xdvdatwks`, and `http://bit.ly/xdvdatwks2`.

Citrix® StoreFront™ tweaks

In most cases, you should not need to tweak the StoreFront application. Here are some tweaks to help improve performance.

HTML5

One tweak worth mentioning for StoreFront is to enable HTML5 on StoreFront, to be used in combination with the latest HTML5-enabled Citrix Receiver.

CRL checking

Certificate revocation list checking is when the StoreFront server checks the certificate revocation for its locally signed files, which can add significant delay before the login page is displayed. You can disable this, and speed up the user experience.

To disable CRLChecking on StoreFront, perform the following steps on the StoreFront server(s):

1. Log in as administrator.
2. Open a PowerShell command window.
3. Run these PowerShell commands.

   ```
   Add-PSSnapin Citrix.DeliveryServices.Framework.Commands
   Set-DSAssemblyVerification $false
   ```

4. Open a text editor such as Notepad, and edit the file placed at `c:\Windows\Microsoft.NET\Framework\v4.0.30319\aspnet.config`.
5. Under `<runtime>`, add the line for `<generatePublisherEvidence enabled="false" />`
6. Save the file
7. Do the same thing for the 64 bit version file placed at `c:\Windows\Microsoft.NET\Framework64\v4.0.30319\aspnet.config`.
8. Run **IISRESET** to apply the changes.

[Tribal Knowledge says to repeat the preceding procedure on other Citrix servers that run IIS, such as Studio.]

Disable NetBIOS

It may not improve performance, but it is definitely an unnecessary component, you can disable NetBIOS on the StoreFront server. To disable NetBIOS on the StoreFront server, perform the following steps on the StoreFront server(s):

1. Log in as administrator.
2. Open the **Network Interface Adapter** properties.
3. Click on **Advanced** under the properties for **TCP/IP version 4**.
4. Click on the **WINS** tab and disable **NetBIOS over TCP/IP**.

Socket pooling

Enabling socket pooling on StoreFront allows it to create and maintain a pool of sockets for connections instead of having to create them on the fly when users connect. This improves performance, especially for SSL connections. To enable socket pooling on StoreFront, perform the following steps:

1. Log on as administrator.
2. Edit the `web.config` file, located at `c:\inetpub\wwwroot\Citrix\<storename>`
3. Change the **pooledSockets="on"** setting.
4. Run **IISRESET** to apply the changes

Application Initialization

In Windows Server 2008 R2, 2012, and 2012 R2 there is a feature that allows applications to be always running in an application pool in IIS. The feature is called Application Initialization. Application Initialization for IIS 7.5 and above enables you to improve the responsiveness of applications by proactively loading and initializing the application, dependencies, and databases before the first user request arrives.

Application Initialization is built in to IIS 8.0. You will need to install it for IIS 7.5 at `http://www.iis.net/downloads/microsoft/application-initialization`.

To enable Application Initialization on the StoreFront server:

1. Log in as administrator.

2. Launch Internet Information Services Manager.

3. In the **Connections** pane, open the server and site containing the Citrix application and select it.

4. In the **Action** pane, click **Configure** under the **Manage WCF and WF Services** heading.

5. In the **Configure WCF and WF for Application**, click on **Auto-Start**.

6. In the **Auto-Start** dialog box, click on **Enabled** to enable auto-start for all services in the application.

7. If a dialog box pops up asking you to set the application to **Always Running**, click on **Yes** to set **startMode** to **AlwaysRunning**.

8. Run **IISRESET** to apply the changes

There are a couple of config files you can check to make sure the changes were made by performing the following steps:

1. Open the `%windir%\system32\inetsrv\config\applicationHost.config` file.

2. Locate the `/configuration/system.applicationHost/applicationPools` setting.

3. For all of your Citrix applications, you should see the parameter `startMode="AlwaysRunning"`.

4. Locate the `/configuration/system.applicationHost/sites` setting.

5. For all of your Citrix applications you should see the parameter `preloadEnabled="true"`.

Citrix® Studio tweaks

When considering Studio performance tweaks, study the following:

Database split

If you are running a XenDesktop site of any size, you may want to split the logging and monitoring databases. To split the databases, perform the following steps:

1. Log in as administrator.
2. Open Citrix Studio.
3. Click on **Configuration** in the left side navigation frame.
4. In the middle frame select the monitoring database.
5. In the right frame select **Change Database**.
6. Do the same for the logging database.

Citrix® Director tweaks

When considering Director performance tweaks, study the following:

Pre-populate domain

You can speed up the login process by pre-populating the domain field. This is a nice tweak and your users will be grateful for this.

To pre-populate the domain field, perform the following steps:

1. Log in as administrator
2. Open a command window or PowerShell window.
3. Open the file placed at `C:\inetpub\wwwroot\Director\Logon.aspx`.
4. Locate the line `<asp:TextBox ID="Domain" runat="server" CssClass="text-box"></asp:TextBox>`.
5. Change it to `<asp:TextBox ID="Domain" runat"server" Text="<Domain name>" CssClass="text-box"></asp:TextBox>`.
6. Run **IISRESET** to apply the changes

Session timeout

The default session timeout is way too long, around four hours. In certain environments, these idle sessions are retained in order to log on quickly for smooth roaming. If you don't need the default timeout you can lower it to keep idle resources from consuming that valuable hardware stack.

To change the session timeout, perform the following steps:

1. Log in as administrator.
2. Open IIS Manager.
3. Browse to `\Sites\Default Web Site\Director` in the left hand navigation frame.
4. Open **Session State** in the right hand navigation frame.
5. Change the **Time-Out (in minutes)** value under **Cookie Settings**.
6. Click **Apply** in **Actions**.
7. Run **IISRESET** to apply the changes.

Citrix® Delivery Controller tweaks

When considering Delivery Controller performance tweaks, study the following.

SQL mirroring

On large XenDesktop sites, you might be creating more than one delivery controller. If that is the case, use SQL mirroring for fast failover. SQL mirroring is all about the high availability of the SQL database. Mirroring works on a per-database level and works with databases that use the full-recovery model. One server acts as the primary or principal server that serves clients, and the other server acts as a hot standby mirror server. Hot standby means rapid failover without data loss.

Database mirroring can use either a synchronous or asynchronous operation. Asynchronous updates hit each database immediately, while synchronous updates hit both databases in synchronization with each database at the cost of latency. Synchronous operation is considered high-safety mode and is more protective of data. Asynchronous operation is considered high-performance as it writes data to each database independently as fast as the data arrives.

Connection Leasing

When Citrix moved from **Independent Management Architecture (IMA)** to the **Flexcast Management Architecture (FMA)** they removed the **Local Host Cache (LHC)** and replaced it with Connection Leasing. Connection Leasing supplements SQL high availability. When it is enabled on the delivery controllers, it caches the users' connections to their recently used applications and desktops, if they are pooled. This is enabled by default.

Note that while Connection Leasing is supposed to provide some level of enhanced availability during a database outage, there is no performance improvement.

The real benefit over LHC is that, if the database becomes unavailable, the **Desktop Delivery Controller (DDC)** enters lease connection mode and replays the cached operations so a user can connect or reconnect to a recently used desktop or application from StoreFront.

 Note that Connection Leasing is specific to XenApp/RDS VDA and is not available in Desktop VDA/VDI.

Separate roles

When Citrix did a large scale (5,000 users) test they created three DDC's and assigned them specific roles. DDC1 was the site master and performed pool management. DDC2 and DDC3 handled VDA registrations and XML brokering. Tribal Knowledge says you can get away with three DDCs serving 8,000 users without separating roles. If you get into a large deployment of 10,000 or more users, you may need to separate the DDC into specific roles.

 The 5,000 user test report can be found at http://bit.ly/xdp5k.

Citrix® License Server tweaks

Always run the Citrix License Server on its own virtual machine. On small to medium sized XenDesktop sites, the license server won't be much of an issue. When you get into large deployments, you will need to scale appropriately. Early tests indicate that a Citrix License Server can issue approximately 170 licenses per second or 306,000 licenses every 30 minutes.

Also be aware that the license server is available as a virtual appliance separately and you can also run Citrix licensing as a service on a Windows server.

Active Directory tweaks

For best performance, you should run Microsoft Active Directory on a dedicated virtual machine. Tribal Knowledge says that it wouldn't hurt to keep the domain controller on a physical server to remove dependency on the hypervisor in case it fails.

Disable forest searching

By default, Director performs a forest-wide search of the logged in admin and Director machine's domain. As you start to scale up your XenDesktop site, Active Directory might slow you down, because, by default, all of the global catalogs for the Active Directory forest are searched with **Lightweight Directory Access Protocol (LDAP)**. It is best to turn this off.

To disable AD **Forest Searching**, perform the following steps:

1. Log in as administrator.
2. Open IIS Manager.
3. Browse to \Sites\Default Web Site\Director in the left hand navigation frame.
4. Select **Application Settings**.
5. Add a new value called **ActiveDirectory.ForestSearch**. Select **Value** as **false**.
6. Click **Apply** in **Actions**.
7. Run **IISRESET** to apply the changes.

DHCP and DNS

XenDesktop uses DHCP and DNS services. Most installations use Microsoft DHCP and DNS, but it can work with other vendor solutions. In terms of performance, you should run the DHCP and DNS services on dedicated virtual machines. You can run Active Directory, DHCP, and DNS on the same machine as a proof of concept, but when you get into production you will want to separate these out into their own virtual machines.

SQL databases

There are some improvements to SQL that coincide with the release of XenDesktop 7.x:

- Use SQL mirroring because it has the fastest failover (Database HA)
- Use **AlwaysOn Availability Groups**
- Use SQL clustering (Server HA)
- You must be sysadmin to create SQL databases automatically through Studio
- Enable **Read-Committed Snapshots** on the SQL server database

Please note that you wouldn't necessarily use mirroring and clustering together, you could choose one or the other. SQL mirroring is a technology that increases the high availability of the database by mirroring the databases. SQL clustering is a technology that provides high availability for the entire SQL server instance and is built and installed on top of Windows server failover clusters.

Citrix Provisioning Services™

Citrix Provisioning Services (**PVS**) allows computers to be provisioned and re-provisioned in real time from a single shared-disk image. In doing so, administrators can completely eliminate the need to manage and patch individual systems. Instead, all image management is done on the master image. The local hard disk drive of each system may be used for runtime data caching or, in some scenarios, removed from the system entirely, which reduces power usage, system failure rates, and security risks.

Using provisioning services, administrators prepare a device (a master target device) for imaging by installing the required software on that device. A vDisk image is then created from the master target device's hard drive and saved to the network (on a provisioning server or storage device).

Provisioning server was going to be end of life and replaced by Machine Creation Services. Having said that, provisioning server is still very popular.

Spanning Tree

Disable Spanning Tree and enable Port-Fast or Fast-Link. The amount of time it takes to converge the switch network might be too long and cause the **Pre-boot Execution Environment** (**PXE**) to time out.

Large Send Offload

Segmenting and storing packets to send in large frames causes latency and timeouts to the provisioning server. This should be disabled on all provisioning servers and clients. To disable Large Send Offload, open the **Network Interface Card** (**NIC**) properties and select the **Advanced** tab.

Auto negotiation

Auto negotiation requires network devices and their switches to negotiate a speed before communication begins. This can cause long starting times and PXE timeouts, especially when starting multiple target devices with different NIC speeds. Citrix recommends hardcoding all provisioning server ports (server and client) on the NIC and on the switch.

Stream service isolation

New advancements in network infrastructure, such as 10 GB networking, may not require the stream service to be isolated from other traffic. If security is of primary concern, then Citrix recommends isolating or segmenting the PVS stream traffic from other production traffic. However, in many cases, isolating the stream traffic can lead to a more complicated networking configuration and actually decrease network performance in some cases.

Summary

XenDesktop Virtual Desktop Infrastructure is a complex menagerie of equipment and software. As with any solution like this of any size, unless you understand all of the component parts, you will end up with mediocre performance. Improving performance can only be done while actually measuring performance. After reading this book, you should have a solid grasp of all of the moving parts of XenDesktop deployment. If you haven't already started, you can now start to diagram and plan your XenDesktop site, with a head start on what performance tweaks you will consider making along the way, and where. I hope you have enjoyed reading the book and now have some new ideas about how to address performance when it comes to designing and implementing your XenDesktop site. Keep this book with you as you move along. Be sure to visit the project accelerator at `http://bit.ly/xdprj`, and review the latest design guide at `http://bit.ly/xdhandbk`.

Index

Thank you for buying
Optimizing Citrix® XenDesktop® for High Performance

About Packt Publishing

Packt, pronounced 'packed', published its first book, *Mastering phpMyAdmin for Effective MySQL Management*, in April 2004, and subsequently continued to specialize in publishing highly focused books on specific technologies and solutions.

Our books and publications share the experiences of your fellow IT professionals in adapting and customizing today's systems, applications, and frameworks. Our solution-based books give you the knowledge and power to customize the software and technologies you're using to get the job done. Packt books are more specific and less general than the IT books you have seen in the past. Our unique business model allows us to bring you more focused information, giving you more of what you need to know, and less of what you don't.

Packt is a modern yet unique publishing company that focuses on producing quality, cutting-edge books for communities of developers, administrators, and newbies alike. For more information, please visit our website at www.packtpub.com.

About Packt Enterprise

In 2010, Packt launched two new brands, Packt Enterprise and Packt Open Source, in order to continue its focus on specialization. This book is part of the Packt Enterprise brand, home to books published on enterprise software – software created by major vendors, including (but not limited to) IBM, Microsoft, and Oracle, often for use in other corporations. Its titles will offer information relevant to a range of users of this software, including administrators, developers, architects, and end users.

Writing for Packt

We welcome all inquiries from people who are interested in authoring. Book proposals should be sent to author@packtpub.com. If your book idea is still at an early stage and you would like to discuss it first before writing a formal book proposal, then please contact us; one of our commissioning editors will get in touch with you.

We're not just looking for published authors; if you have strong technical skills but no writing experience, our experienced editors can help you develop a writing career, or simply get some additional reward for your expertise.

Getting Started with XenDesktop® 7.x

ISBN: 978-1-84968-976-2   Paperback: 422 pages

Deliver desktops and applications to your end users, anywhere, anytime, with XenDesktop® 7.x.

1. Build a complete and secure XenDesktop 7 site from the ground up.

2. Discover how to virtualize and deliver accessible desktops and applications to your end users.

3. Full of clear, step-by-step instructions with screenshots, which will walk you through the entire process of site creation.

Citrix XenDesktop 5.6 Cookbook

ISBN: 978-1-84968-504-7   Paperback: 354 pages

Implement a fully featured XenDesktop 5.6 architecture in a rich and powerful VDI experience configuration

1. Real-world methodologies and functioning explanations about the XenDesktop 5.6 architecture and its satellite components used to perform a service-oriented architecture.

2. Learn how to publish desktops and applications to end user devices, optimizing their performance and increasing the general security.

Please check **www.PacktPub.com** for information on our titles

Instant Citrix XenDesktop 5 Starter

ISBN: 978-1-78217-002-0   Paperback: 66 pages

Your step-by-step guide to building a full-fledged XenDesktop infrastructure from scratch

1. Learn something new in an Instant! A short, fast, focused guide delivering immediate results.

2. Know how to install XenDesktop, integrate it with PVS and build streamed and pooled desktops.

3. Learn how to build provisioning servers, capture VHD files, and configure streaming.

Mastering Citrix® XenDesktop®

ISBN: 978-1-78439-397-7   Paperback: 484 pages

Design and implement a high performance and efficient virtual desktop infrastructure using Citrix® XenDesktop®

1. Design, deploy, configure, optimize, troubleshoot, and maintain XenDesktop for enterprise environments and to meet emerging high-end business requirements.

2. Configure Citrix XenDesktop to deliver a rich virtual desktop experience to end users.

3. A comprehensive, practical guide to monitoring a XenDesktop environment and automating XenDesktop tasks using PowerShell.

Please check **www.PacktPub.com** for information on our titles